# Letting Go, Moving On

### Nikki Simos

First published by Busybird Publishing 2016

Copyright © 2016 Nikki Simos

ISBN: 978-0-9945728-6-8

Nikki Simos has asserted her right under the Copyright, Designs and Patents Act 1988 to be identified as the author of this work. The information in this book is based on the author's experiences and opinions. The publisher specifically disclaims responsibility for any adverse consequences, which may result from use of the information contained herein. Permission to use information has been sought by the author. Any breaches will be rectified in further editions of the book.

All rights reserved. No part of this publication may be reproduced, stored in or introduced into a retrieval system, or transmitted in any form, or by any means (electronic, mechanical, photocopying, recording or otherwise) without the prior written permission of the author. Any person who does any unauthorised act in relation to this publication may be liable to criminal prosecution and civil claims for damages. Enquiries should be made through the publisher.

**Cover image**: Richard Trembath

**Cover design**: Busybird Publishing

**Layout and typesetting**: Busybird Publishing

**Editor**: Beau Hillier

Busybird Publishing
PO Box 855
Eltham Victoria
Australia 3095

www.busybird.com.au

# Contents

| | | |
|---|---|---|
| About the Author | | 1 |
| Gratitude and Acknowledgements | | 3 |
| Introduction | | 5 |
| 1. | Faith, Love and Light | 15 |
| 2. | Parents and Pride | 23 |
| 3. | Unwanted Attention | 31 |
| 4. | Awareness of Spiritual Senses | 51 |
| 5. | High School Motives and Emotives | 61 |
| 6. | Vipassana, Woori Yallock | 71 |
| Conclusion | | 87 |

## About the Author

Nikki Simos has a multidisciplinary Bachelor of Arts, a Diploma in Secondary Education and a Diploma in Advanced Psychology and Counselling. She has a Neuro-Linguistic Programming Coaching Certification that includes hypnotherapy, life coaching and NLP Coaching.

Nikki has over 30 years' experience working in public sector services such as film and television, telecommunication, retail and children's entertainment. She once worked for a member of parliament and continues to work as a specialist teacher and a coach, counsellor and mentor. She actively functions as a motivational speaker, sharing stories and meaningful insights on how to live a life of happiness and where you can find it, even when you think you may be at the end of your rope.

# *Gratitude and Acknowledgements*

Thanks to my wonderful, supportive and loving family. My husband Con. My beautiful respectful children Yiannis, Vangelis and Alexia Simos. My father, Ioannis Selimis, and my sisters, Tina and Smaro. Also to my niece and nephews and my mother-in-law. I know that my secrets have perhaps opened up conversations you would never have imagined, and I also know that my experiences are the past, and I only wish that you can learn from them.

I thank you all for your understanding during the occasions when time was not provided for you, as my prime focus was writing my memoirs. Although you were hesitant about me unleashing my past upon the world and concerned about the implications – the perceptions, the judgements, the comments that may arise – just know that my intention was to seek healing, forgiveness, relief and clarity. I can only hope that these attributes will become a part of different areas in your lives – in your careers, your relationships and your spirituality.

With confidence and without regret, I can now honestly say and believe that I am who I need to be, even as I continue to grow into a better version of myself. Thank you with greatest gratitude and respect from your mother, daughter, sister and auntie.

# Introduction

I was born on 8 March 1972, in the heart of East Melbourne. A true Aussie, based on my birthplace in Mercy Hospital. However, I was baptised in Greece at the age of two in Lalysos, on the beautiful Greek island of Rhodes.

My late mother, who died at sixty-nine years of age on 29 May 2012, always made reference to how I was born and she would say, 'You were a hard baby to get out because you came out sideways, like half the moon.'

As my late mother was un-educated and hadn't completed any formal academic education, although she'd attended primary school until Grade 3, she married at nineteen years of age to my father Ioannis Selimis.

My mother's family consisted of eleven brothers and sisters, five girls and six boys. Mother left the popular Greek island of Rhodes and came to Australia where she met my idol: my father. Most people referred to him as John.

Sevasmia, my mother's birth name, often spoke of things as best she could describe in her own unique manner. Sometimes she would make sense and sometimes she would make no sense, yet we always knew that everything she wanted to say had a message. Usually, she would have a focus on house cleaning. That was something my mother was really good at: cleaning, cooking and ironing.

Sevasmia gave birth to four children and sadly one was a miscarriage. The first child was the lost boy; then Constantina was born, named after my father's mother; then Smaragthi, who was named after my mother's mother; and then me. I was named after my grandfather on my dad's side – instead of Niko, I was named Nikoletta and converted over time to Nikki.

Right up until today this complicated things for me, especially when it came to completing forms for passports, my driver's licence and other legal documentation. Previously my details on paper were broken down from Nikoletta to Nikki/Nicole, so I altered it to Nikki and left it at that. It has all been sorted to date, thank goodness.

My father was really hoping for a boy to be born in order to take over the family name – obviously this was not the case. My father once told us girls that when I was born, he recalls asking the nurse if 'it', referring to me, was a boy. My father was taken aback a little by the news I was a girl and apparently, he remembers walking out of the theatre room disappointed, yet pleased to know that his wife was well after my birth.

That very thought of my father being disappointed that I was born a girl and not a boy played with my self-esteem for a few years as a young child. Over the years, the story would keep repeating itself and coming up amongst family and my siblings.

I manifested a belief that in order for my father to give me unconditional love, and to be worthy and valued in my family unit, I had to do things better than anybody else. This is how I would know that I would be noticed, valued and loved by my parents. I wanted to stand out in the crowd.

Today, I know that my father is very proud of me and my successes. I also know in his heart that he has me placed as his favourite girl, yet he would never admit this publicly, simply to keep the harmony and to not create jealousy amongst us girls in our family. Not that this would happen, as we aim to have peace between the three of us – well, to the best of our abilities.

I can truly say I have worked in many industries. My first job was at the age of twelve, when I worked every Saturday morning for five hours in the local delicatessens. I remember receiving my first cash payment of $17.50. I worked at the deli in Preston Market for seven years, only on Saturday mornings, and was eventually able to save enough money to purchase my first car: a red Telstar. When I reached the age of seventeen, I enrolled in university and was accepted at the Western Institute in St Albans, which is now a Victoria University campus.

I was fortunate to receive a placement at university, as the member of parliament that I was working with part-time was friends with the dean of the university – otherwise, I don't know if I would've been successful enough to get into university, with the results that I had to work with from completing Year 12.

While working part-time for the member of parliament, I ceased my employment with the deli and commenced work with a swimming centre as the front desk person. This was for a short term. I was in charge of taking payment from parents and selling lollies and chips to the children after their swimming lesson.

As time went on I ceased employment from the swimming centre located in Tullamarine. I continued to work for a member of parliament for four years, and then I began to volunteer my time with a not-for-profit organisation and was one of the founders of the Melbourne Community Television Station (Channel 31).

This is where my love for film and television began. I desperately wanted a career in the field. I volunteered my time for a period of seven years and then was fortunate to gain contract employment with the Australian Broadcasting Corporation, Channel 7, Channel 9 and Channel 10.

I had experience working on various pre-production and production stages of the following programs in the late 80s and early 90s: *Neighbours, Young Talent Time, The Damnation of Harvey McHugh* and *Phoenix*.

In this period of my life, I also studied part-time at the Judy Banks School of Television, the Jan Sheedy School of Grooming and the Johnny Young Talent School. My father would travel from Broadmeadows all the way to Richmond once a week for me to attend these extra-curricular activities.

These schools and institutions were working with now-celebrities, back in the days when Kylie Minogue, Dannii Minogue, Guy Pearce, Craig McLachlan, Vince Deltito, Joe Perrone and Karen Knowles were not famous yet.

I never imagined knowing people in my past who would become famous, and I'd never have imagined that I would never have been remembered. I guess I have always been busy keeping in the background and working hard.

After years passing, I also worked in the telecommunication industry for Telstra. I had worked for Medibank, Bras 'n Things, Furniture Galore (in Campbellfield) and IGA in supervisory roles.

I completed my multidisciplinary Bachelor of Arts with Victoria University of Technology in 1994; I also competed a course in modern Greek at Melbourne University in 1994. I got married in the same year, and began my sole trading business as a children's entertainer, which I successfully did for ten years as 'Nix the Clown'. In that time I had two beautiful boys with my soul mate.

I returned to La Trobe University in 2007 to complete my Secondary Education qualification. I completed studies successfully and gave birth to our third child, a girl.

I was then successfully employed as a generalist teacher full-time in 2008. During this time I completed other certifications and improved my understanding of literacy, Auslan (signing for the deaf) and music.

In 2014, I commenced my part-time sole trading business as a coach, counsellor, mentor and motivational public speaker.

I completed my Neuro-Linguistic Programming Certification, Time Line Therapy Certification, Life Coaching Certification and a Diploma in Counselling. I also completed over 500 hours of coaching; although a lot of that had been pro bono, a few clients were actually paying clients.

For the first year of my business, like in all new businesses, there was more outlay of funds than receiving funds. My husband would focus on the monetary gain and outlay. It became an issue for me because he could never understand the idea of doing things for love, with a passion and driven by a genuine cause. My husband is very auditory and digital, so everything is facts, data and results driven. I only came to realise this after starting NLP Coaching.

Having this understanding broadened my horizons and allowed me to understand people and the thinking behind their actions and emotions.

In December 2015, I decided to change career paths once more and for the final time, to lead me into a retirement position and hopefully set up my family for life. I would continue to grow my business as a coach, counsellor and mentor, and I've also considered becoming a councillor working for local government and supporting the community, country and people with issues that matter to me and need to be addressed.

As the outcome was always uncertain, and the choices I made giving no guarantees of employment, I couldn't be sure what other doors and opportunities would come about.

My life experiences have certainly completed a full circle. What I thought I could never do, I made a commitment and decided to do. Crazy, I know.

Getting back to my parents, my father John has strong values and believes that all girls should be treated fairly and the same, with everything provided to us right up to the day he dies and beyond. He wishes for us to continue this belief within our own families and generations to come.

I think I am continuing to do a good job of that when I speak to my three children and emphasise the beliefs and values that I have about family and equality.

He loves all his children and would do absolutely anything in his power to provide support, care and love for us. And at the age of seventy-five, he displays the same compassion for his grandchildren and sons-in-law. God bless him!

I mentioned earlier that my father is my idol. I say this with complete certainty and belief. My father is the kindest and most supportive, wise and knowledgeable man. He has travelled 176 countries during his life journey. My father was employed as a sea merchant and cruised day by day, night by night, week by week and sometimes even month upon month on varied transporting merchant ships over the years. His amazing journey also needs to be written and I cannot wait to write his story. I have to keep reminding myself, one step at a time.

I must admit that it is through his strength, guidance, wisdom, hardship and experiences that I bring myself to finally write my first memoir, *Letting Go, Moving On*.

I am who I am today because of my father's strength, which he has truly embedded in me.

He has shown me courage – to fear nothing, stand up and speak for what you believe is righteous, and become all that you can be.

He has been my ultimate hero and has demonstrated how to sustain strong beliefs and values in all areas of my life and maintain positivity, creativity and a healthy mindset.

My father has experienced immense hardships in his life and he has clearly demonstrated for me what perseverance means, and how to continue to live long and prosper, as Spock from *Star Trek* would say.

Along with my father's support, love, compassion and belief in me, I have also come into faith again. I've begun to develop a relationship with God and an awareness of His love, support and compassion for me.

I am beginning to understand the willpower of God's word, and the Holy Spirit and how this has had (and continues to have) an impact on my life. I will endeavour to share more of this insight in this book.

In writing this book, I aim to reach out to you and create an awareness and understanding that success is measured differently for everyone. Our journeys are unique and well worth mentioning and sharing, for greater learning for all.

I aim to clearly identify what it means to become all that you can be and how it is possible to do so, regardless of any challenges that you experience in life.

I aim to explain why it is imperative that you understand your challenges and how to create the determination to continue on and never give up, offering forgiveness for all that has been said and done in all areas of our lives – as I have done, specifically in my life.

I aim to inspire you in moving towards your dreams and aspirations, without holding back for any reasons that you may be presented with in your journey.

So who am I and why have I chosen to write this book for you?

Simply put, I, like many of us, have a story to tell.

I believe my story, like yours, is unique. When you come to understand all the experiences and decisions made over your lifetime, you come to a point when you feel you are destined to share all that you know for others to grow.

People who know me well will let you know that I always have a story to tell from the various experiences that I've had. Therefore, I figured that if my stories add entertainment, valuable lessons and insightfulness to people's lives, then I have a duty of care to complete this mission as part of my journey. I have written about my personal stories and will continue to tell them to the best of my ability, while I am alive and can do so, therefore leaving a legacy to my children and future grandchildren.

I believe that we are all born with a purpose in life. The difficult thing for us as humans and mortal souls is to figure out what that purpose is.

I have discovered a new higher purpose that a significant someone has for me. Someone I believe in, I can abide in, I can trust in – who I can ask for guidance to assist me with true fellowship. I can ask for forgiveness and know that I am forgiven because I feel the love given back into my life today.

Yes, you may have guessed – that significant someone is God!

Now, you may put this book down right this minute and say

to yourself, is this person part of a ministry? The answer is no (at least not yet).

Is this person a bible fanatic? The answer is no.

Do I want you to discover what's best for you? Yes, I do – and the earlier in life you achieve this, the better. What I want you to say yes to, is knowing what is right for you.

Every one of us is unique and has different experiences. What you choose to believe in that is greater than you is truly your decision to make, when you discover what the higher source is for you, what appeals to you and what feels right for you.

We are all born and destined to die – our lives are simply a journey.

# Faith, Love and Light

I've decided that my life and journey is in God's hands and He will decide for me what I will experience in order to learn from. He helps me to grow as a person and contribute to all that I can, serving and supporting others more than myself.

I believe I have always been aware of this, but have chosen never to embrace it beforehand. It has taken me forty-three years to understand the concept of the choices that I make, the direction that I take and the outcomes of my actions. I can be driven by my own thoughts.

In contrast to all of the 'I' thoughts, I have chosen to believe in the Holy Spirit, the Lord and Jesus Christ. I pray every day, every moment for His word, His directions, His actions and thoughts. Through His willpower, invested in my mindset, He will guide me and take me to places that I would never have imagined.

And so, my new journey begins. I have already encountered

and embraced this new journey and now I am ready to share it with you.

*

We must come to realise that we are all unique and we all have a purpose. Our road map is already worked out for us. There is a Greek saying: *'I mira mass enai grameni'*, which translates to 'our journey has already been written for us'.

My understanding of this is that I would be actively His child and my mortal soul will do His work of greatness through me in supporting, nurturing, sharing, contributing, growing and giving to others. My purpose is to ensure that they become the best version of themselves, which is ultimately what God wants for all humanity on this planet, living a life of peace and harmony on a greater scale.

When we are searching and requesting a response to an event, we do ask and seek answers. We generally seek it from a higher source or energy, so why not God?

I know that we all speak out His name. Especially when something goes terribly wrong in our lives and we say things like, 'God, why me?' 'Why now?' 'Why my mother, father, brother or sister?' 'God, please help me,' or the classic spoken words, 'Oh my God, what on earth …'

I have come to believe that God's word is pure, and the truth is written as scripture in the Bible. I have discovered that the Bible provides us with an understanding of past experiences that have been recorded, and have become linked with our ways of living where life can be fruitful for us all. There are explanations here that can give us perspective.

Only recently have I come to understand that we had an Old Testament and New Testament, and each prophet or saint had their stories to tell via their own enlightenments and personal experiences. That understanding alone, for me, was a breakthrough.

As I continue to expose myself to scriptures in the New Testament, I will continue to further my understanding of God's word and faith, having completed a catechism interactive workshop offered by the Greek Orthodox Archdiocese of Australia. My aim to understand the orthodox religion has offered a unique and rich learning experience for me.

People choose to believe in different universal energies and extremities, and I respect that completely. However, by entering and embracing the understanding of the relationship that you can discover with Jesus, you find yourself wanting more of Jesus and the Holy Spirit within your soul. In my opinion, this enlightenment is a truly amazing feeling throughout the mind, body and soul, and all you could ever want to feel complete as an individual. It is awesome!

I also have come to understand that if we all have no sense of purpose in living our life, and we don't have clarity on what our mission in life is meant to be, we are likely to fall into a trap and feel stuck. We may be led by entities that offer deception, such as Satan.

We all end up just living without knowing any more than our daily chores that we have always done. Therefore, we repeat what we already know and become hesitant to explore anything new or unknown. Fear and uncertainty take over; feelings and thoughts of not being good enough take over.

This is what holds us back. We allow ourselves to feel stuck and become something we are not. We immediately lose self-esteem, confidence and self-belief, which is why it is crucial to recognise that becoming a better version of yourself is not just your own thinking, but guided by love and the presence of Jesus in your life when you allow your soul to enter into that realm of the unknown.

In becoming better versions of ourselves and doing this all with the presence of Jesus in our lives, as He has already written our paths for us all, why choose another way?

Follow God's way. Follow the way that will guarantee all the success, all the love, all the wealth, all the greatness, all the peace and harmony you could ever want in your lives. Offer unconditional love for yourself and others and receive the Holy Spirit for all that it is worth – and, in fact, it is worth our lives.

I firmly believe that we all have to trust in Jesus and go with the feelings, visions and hearings that come through us all, ensuring we trust the experiences and not become hesitant or afraid to explore further.

When you experience such powerful internal emotions, and I have, it completely transforms your thinking because it is guided by genuine love.

The butterfly feelings in your gut, the tingling sensations, the white light images and thoughts that are filtered through your mind, and sometimes the sounds that you come to hear via meditation – that, my friends, is from real goal-setting. That is God's calling, advising you and guiding you with all His power within you, setting you on a purposeful mission that you can resonate with.

As you will discover further into my story, I have experienced this overabundance of emotions, with new beginnings and adventures that I would've never imagined before.

I firmly believe that God will always help us get on the path to where we need to go. He as our Father is gentle and kind and wants the best for us all. He has never turned his back on us and we simply need to ask for His help and He is already there for us all. Loving us unconditionally, looking out for us and hoping that we notice his pathway and journey for us, when we choose to follow that path and embrace our Father and all that He has to offer. Amen to that Glory and may the Lord have mercy on our souls.

In Romans 8:6, the Bible scripture states, 'The mind governed by the flesh is death, but the mind governed by the Spirit is life and peace.'

I have come to understand that when I have a thought in my mind, I have created a habit that I always ask God first and then feel the Holy Spirit working within my soul, creating a sense of what feels right to continue on with. This is different to speaking with your inner voice and listening to the inner ego, which may offer alternative deceptive ideas to follow on with.

Unless you believe, have faith, feel and see for yourself it may be difficult to understand and come to terms with what I am suggesting.

It is this true enlightenment that I have experienced that has allowed me to write my memoirs and feel the freedom, confidence and courage to become all that I am today and all that I can be tomorrow.

*

I asked the question earlier, who am I? I am still aiming to answer that to the best of my ability.

On the surface level, I am a mother of three beautiful children, two boys and one girl. I have a wonderful, supportive soul mate as my husband and we have been successfully married for nineteen years to date. We have no doubt that we will grow old and humble together because we have honest communication and a strong connection between us. There is not a day that goes by where we don't state that we love and value each other. We have moments, don't get me wrong – there have been times where we haven't spoken to each other for some days. Yet we always aim to understand each other, communicate and let go so we can move on to the next step, drawing us both together once again.

We live on a quarter-acre in a town named Wallan. I often refer to it as Pretty Sally as that is how I saw it advertised when I first stumbled across our residence, now ten years ago. We own a beautiful golden retriever named Archie, two goldfish and two birds that my daughter named Elser and Fluffy Lemon (who unfortunately passed away in December 2015).

I will mention that most of my inspiration and learning does come from people who have walked the walk and do the talk and are great leaders in their own right. You will also discover that my journey has been full of experiences and decisions that had to be made in order to move away from bad events and place me back on track.

My influences have been celebrities like Oprah, Deepak Chopra, Tony Robbins, Nelson Mandela and Ghandi – and I am still learning about God and His influence on me.

I want to thank you in advance for allowing me the opportunity to have my world intertwined with yours, supporting you with setting new goals and committing to becoming the best version of you, whatever that looks like in your world and your reality.

Sometimes, just knowing that someone else may have experienced something very similar to you is a breath of fresh air. You discover that you can move on and keep going until you grow and become a better version of yourself. This is a new beginning that leads towards new inspirations in the journey that we all experience.

*

When we are facing difficult circumstances that have no meaning to us, or situations are out of our control, we seek the help and guidance from God and we all to tend to ask, 'Why, God? Why me, why now? What do I need to do to make this right? Help me, guide me – share with me a feeling, a thought, and I will follow.'

When we don't know why occurrences happen and why challenges come about in our lives, we often ask God to guide us with some sort of sign so that we can have a reason, an answer or a better understanding of why things happen.

Coming into the Orthodox Christian faith was a huge mind shift for me. I had to understand for myself what this meant. What is God? Who was Jesus? I was learning to understand how to read a Bible and aiming to understand the Scriptures. I was to become a sponge, soaking in as much information as I could. The challenge was to store it in my memory bank.

I attended different church groups. Pentecostal, Christian Orthodox, Greek Orthodox, Christian Baptist, Presbyterian, Uniting Church – all very interesting learning, with discoveries that I wouldn't have understood if I hadn't allowed myself to go on this journey, embracing it all and being motivated to learn more.

To date, I can say that I am Christian Orthodox and that I belong to a church and attend the Greek Orthodox services as often as I can. My focus is on the Scriptures, and understanding the Old Testament and the New Testament. It's about understanding what has been written and how you make sense of it in your world and your reality. I particularly enjoy the iconography and the tempera art that is involved in such unique creations.

# Parents and Pride

My parents migrated to Australia in 1964 with nothing and officially became Australian citizens in 1968. No finances behind them, no house to live in, no jobs to work at, and one family group to associate themselves with. The good thing is that my parents had each other, and managed to stay married for forty-eight years until Mum sadly passed away. My parents had to find a way to live and integrate into this new world that was foreign to them at the time.

My father, Ioannis Selimis, was a sea merchant officer, cleaning and scrubbing the decks and assisting as a cook in the kitchen. He wanted to go to school and finish his third year, primary level; unfortunately for him, he had to support his parents and was requested to work, as his parents couldn't afford to send him to school and provide for his family of seven siblings at the same time.

My mother, Sevasmia Makris (her maiden name) was uneducated. She was brought up to be the stereotypical

Greek girl who had to cook, clean, wash clothes and complete house duties all day every day. For my mother, marrying my father in Australia was a blessing; it was her escape from doing all that she had to for her family that included eleven siblings. She had the opportunity to think about doing the things she was great at for her own family.

When my parents got married in 1964, not long after they settled in Australia, they began a family. Mum had four children, but sadly had a miscarriage about ten weeks into her first pregnancy.

The second child my mother had was Constantina. My parents shortened her name to Tina and that remained. She was referred to as the troublemaker and the little devil. She was a rebel in her teenage years, got up to all sorts of mischief and was Mum and Dad's challenge for years. She could write her own memoirs with all her experiences.

Then mother gave birth to the third child, Smaragthi. We referred to her as Smaro. This was a popular name for our family as there were lots of Smaros in Greece and only three of them that we knew of in Australia. She was born at Mornington and was fair-haired with blue eyes. She was branded the quiet one in our family, and achieved lots in her own little special way. Today she continues to follow that pattern of behaviour that she manifested as a young child.

Finally I was born, initially named Nikoletta and then condensed to Nikki. When I was born in 1972, in the heart of East Melbourne at the Mercy Hospital, my father was really hoping for a boy for someone to carry the family name. He was hoping for a Niko to be born, as this was the name of his father and our grandfather – obviously this wasn't the case.

Over time my father and mother worked in various jobs in order to sustain an income for us to survive and reside permanently in Australia.

Luckily for my sisters and me, we were born in Australia, therefore we were automatically Australian citizens.

My parents' first taste of employment was owning a fish 'n chip shop in Mornington. As Dad provided food for his family back in Greece and also was a fisherman, this was the easiest job that he already knew how to do well. Mum worked in there for a while until she fell pregnant with her fourth child. They then gave it away. Having one young girl running around a fish 'n chip shop and one newborn was going to be difficult to manage for both my parents.

Dad then went into the taxi business as a driver. He did this for some years and as we got older he would share some really interesting stories, like the time a passenger left a bag in his taxi after an early morning pick-up from St Kilda Road. There was $600 and medication sitting in that bag. Dad was an honest man – as much as he knew how this could support his family, he gave it to the police. The police advised him that if no one had come forward after two weeks, then he could claim the money as his own. Two weeks passed and Dad hadn't heard anything back from the police. Therefore, he thought that someone claimed it or the police claimed it for themselves. Dad never knew what the outcome was, until he unexpectedly and to his surprise received lotto tickets in the mail.

My mother was the traditional housewife after having us three girls and worked part-time ironing – while Dad worked night shifts she would iron clothes after putting us all to bed. My parents then decided to change the pace a little.

After two years residing and making ends meet in Australia they were able to save money to travel back overseas to Greece and see how their parents were doing. They contemplated living in Greece again as they saw the hardship that their parents and family members were going through. We were still young enough for my parents to make the decision to stay in Greece or return to Australia; they were split between two countries, two cultures, two different living statuses.

They had to decide to either live in Greece and support their extended family members and us girls or return to Australia, where we would commence school and sustain work but move away from their parents and siblings.

My father decided to return to Australia. He landed a secure job with what was once known as Ansett Australia Airlines, working in the engineering department and cleaning parts of the aeroplane engines.

I remember when Ansett Airlines had promotional family Christmas celebrations and all the employees and family members would attend. There would be rides, show bags and great gift packs for us all. This was lots of fun and I remember Dad being so proud to share his learnings and work with us. The three of us girls thought Dad was an important and valued member at his workplace because we could see that everyone knew 'John'. It was always pleasing to know that.

My mother worked in a factory ironing women's and men's clothing before shipment into stores. She was located in a suburb named Preston on High Street. She also took pride in her work. I remember once when Mum took us all into her workplace because our eldest was too unwell to attend school and she had no one to care for us; Mum asked her boss, known as 'Romio', if it was okay with him for us to be present at work for that day. Romio agreed and actually had us doing some small jobs around the place. We had even been provided with our own 'clock-on card' that you would press into a machine; it would punch holes into the card, indicating your time of arrival on site and your time of departure. I recall inserting my card more than once throughout the day and was fascinated by how the machine knew the time-in and time-out simply from where the holes where made on the imprinted card.

I had an uncle in Australia: my late mother's brother, Uncle

Jimmy. He and his wife Auntie Maria resided in Australia and they had five children. Sadly, Uncle Jimmy passed away in December 2015. We were close with them when we were young and would get together often on weekends for various celebrations. My uncle became a builder and my auntie worked for him as a self-trading business.

This worked out really well for my parents and our family as Uncle Jimmy built our first home in Broadmeadows, on Girgarre Street. It was the first house on that street block and I'm proud to say that most of my memories are in that home.

As years went on, my parents had stable incomes and were able to afford travelling back to Greece every two or three years. Over time my parents travelled back and forth from Australia to Greece seventeen times. I travelled there eleven times, spread out over the years.

I was the odd child in our family as I was the one to be baptised in Greece. My godparents were my mother's parents, which of course were also my grandparents.

I remember three things over the eleven trips that I had to Greece. One is my experience of being baptised at two years old; I recall receiving a grey, soft, thirty centimetre stuffed dog from my godparents after the ceremony. I can clearly remember my grandmother, who was also my godmother. She wore her black apron over her blue jumper and black skirt, with black stockings and her hair tied up in a bun with a net over it. I remember her warm smile as she kindly gave me the only doll they'd ever owned. To this day I have that doggy and it sits on a brown benchtop in my bedroom. It is a short memory of my grandmother, yet a significant one.

I remember when my grandmother had taken me with my mother to the Old Town in Rhodes, which is a popular tourist attraction today, to have my ears pierced for the first time. I remember she arranged for the biggest plain gold circle earrings to be placed into my earlobes.

I don't remember crying but I do remember it hurting.

I also remember when my grandmother took me to the hot baths in Rhodes. It's a public place where people can wash up and bathe. As I was olive-skinned my grandma thought I never washed properly behind my neck and back and took a strong exfoliating scrubber to wash me down with. She rubbed so hard and repeatedly called out, 'Vroma, vroma,' which means dirt, and thought I had never washed myself in that area. My skin was red raw and sensitive after that bath, although I was grateful as I received special attention that day. All because she was my godmother.

The final thing I remember is my grandfather having sex with my grandmother, in this very confined bedroom space upstairs in their home. Although at the time, to me it looked like he was forcing himself onto my godmother and she wanted to move but couldn't. This experience traumatised me for some time. I remember feeling scared, angry and worried for my grandmother yet couldn't tell anyone because you just didn't. I ran away from the house as quickly as I could, pretending that I heard and saw nothing. I guess I attempted to block this memory out as time went by, but some things in life you simply cannot.

I also recall the endless arguments between my relatives that included my grandfather, who I thought looked like Hitler but in a fatter version, arguing about property and who should have the godparents' house after they died. This memory is vivid because I was about ten years of age. Often we would gather around the family home and my late Uncle Jimmy and Auntie Maria would be there along with my godfather, my parents and my sisters. They would sit at a round table, all listening to why my mother had been chosen out of eleven siblings on my mother's side. Discussion would take place about why she was the chosen one to have the house in her name, which then would be given to me as a gift from my godparents.

This argument went on for years. Imagine eleven brothers and sisters all wanting their parents' home after their passing, only to be advised that the house was going to be given to me as a gift from the grandparents because they were my godparents.

I need to explain the importance of providing such a gift and why it held profound significance at the time of these discussions. My grandmother used to be abused, physically and mentally, by my grandfather. I know this because my parents would speak of it only after they passed and my mother's siblings, my other uncle and aunties, would also share the same information.

Therefore, as my parents would travel back to Greece every two years since the age of two for me, the same conversations would repeat over and over again. Conversations about the house, about ownership, about the grandfather being so mean and rough towards my grandmother, and about their dying wishes of wanting to give me the house and have it placed in my name.

What I remember is the round table: the same faces, same arguments and same movements. Nothing changed over the period of time. There were some aunties, my mother's sisters and brothers, who had some personal interest in the house because of its location, based in Ialysos in Rhodes, and because they resided permanently in Greece and we were blow-ins every two years. I didn't understand any of the confrontational discussion at twelve years of age, and now as an adult with family myself I clearly understand the predicaments and selfishness that I have been left to deal with.

Even though my aunties and some uncles had invested interest in the property, as their parents provided a share of the house to them, five out of the six family members involved were happy to hand and sign their share over to me, as this was the wishes of their parents and the remaining siblings didn't want to do so.

As years went by and I grew, understanding more about how best to manage the situation that I was left with, I took on the advice of a solicitor who was based in Old Town, Rhodes and had him work for me as my legal representative in relation to all dealings with the house. I wasn't even thirteen yet and I had already accumulated a massive expense and debt to my name. Great!

The house, I believe, was the death of my mother. I say this because for years all she ever wanted was to have the dying wishes of her parents granted respectfully, honestly and with the best wishes of her siblings. Unfortunately, this was not the case and to this very day I am dealing with the legalities of the house from Australia. I began working and contributing funds towards something that I was hoping to completely own one day, so that I could hand it over to my children and they would have something to own without any implications included.

Ideally, we would have a holiday home and when we could afford to travel to Greece, we would have a place to stay, even though the economy in Greece at present isn't at its best status – but that is another story.

# Unwanted Attention

Where does anyone start with the explanation of unwanted extrasensory attention?

It is imperative to explain to you that my intention in sharing this part of my story is not to defame anyone or seek revenge. I have asked for forgiveness from God for the people involved and I do want to support confidentiality and their reputation with respect to them.

I will refer to alias names and fictional status to reflect the story that must be told. I want to make it clear, however, that I do not forgive the act and no person should experience what I did, ever!

On a deeper level inside my heart and soul, it was this chapter in my life that had to be told in order to support, nurture, serve and save others from experiencing anything alike.

I could have avoided the experience if I wasn't naive and was able to make better choices before the events occurred.

I will explain this statement a little further on.

My first encounter of being raped was when I was at the age of seventeen. I was violated by a minor who was fifteen years of age.

At the time, I was studying full-time at Victoria University, St Albans Campus. I enrolled into a multidisciplinary Bachelor of Arts, specialising and majoring in communication studies, policy studies and sub-majoring in journalism. I attended classes five days a week and spent my Saturday mornings working part-time in a delicatessen. For leisure, I would go to the local swimming centre in Broadmeadows, 3–4 nights a week.

Swimming was my outlet. I loved it. I would immerse myself in the water and feel like I was a dolphin, swimming up to seventy-five laps in a twenty-five metre pool. Today, after three children (and having stopped swimming after that event), I would be lucky if I can complete one lap in a one-metre pool.

I would feel completely relaxed in the environment I was in. I was a regular so the swim guard who worked on the nights that I would swim, named Michael, would also check to see that my swimming techniques were up to scratch and that I wasn't overdoing it.

Michael looked after me and yet he didn't have to, so I thought he was a nice young man. He wanted to become a commander in the Air Force and at the time he was working part-time as the swimming guard instructor. Michael would often switch on the spa for extra time or get more coal for the sauna for me to maximise my workout and get all that I could out of the session for the time I devoted to it.

We became good friends. We even went out for lunch at a park once. I remember sitting down at a park with Michael and we would just chat about life – what we wanted to do and where life was going to take us. Michael used to ride a motorbike. He took me for a ride once and I remember having my VHS camera on the back of it, so I could capture what that would look like and feel like in real time. I recorded this as I was making a promotional video for Honda Motorbike Riding School at the time – and also to have available to broadcast on Melbourne Community Television (Channel 31) as I was one of the founders of the station.

I often found time to get involved with volunteering projects for community services and in my down time I would go to the gym and work out. I saw this as my relaxing, stress relief moments. Away from school, work and people in my life. Time for me.

I was heavily involved in fitness activities after school and I absolutely loved swimming. Unfortunately, my freedom to attend the centre was stripped away from me forever. I made a decision that I was to never go swimming on my own in the local centre again, as a result of the incident that I am about to disclose to you. Never, ever again would I go alone.

It was about 6.30 pm on Thursday evening; daylight savings had already set well into place, which meant it would get dark really quickly during the evenings.

That evening, I remember having a chat with Michael and we were discussing how often he came to the centre and how often he engaged in sporting activities. He was such a nice boy.

At the time, I must admit, I actually didn't mind talking to him and engaging in conversation. What I didn't foresee is what happened next.

That evening after I finished my laps, I felt quite relaxed and tired after a great workout. I wrapped up for the night and got changed, ready to attend to my car and travel the short distance home.

Michael had been standing in the corridor of the swimming centre and it appeared that he was waiting for me. I said hello and asked him what he was still doing there, as he normally would leave way earlier in the evenings.

He asked me if I would be interested in catching up for a drink since I'd finished my workout. I didn't see a problem with that. I could do with a nice warm cuppa as it wasn't late in the evening. I said, 'Okay, let's go up the road for a drink.' We took my car and he suggested that I turn right as he knew of a local café up the road, close by to the football oval.

At this point, I didn't think it was out of the ordinary to follow his request. So I did. We parked the car and got out. We walked towards the little café booth that served tea and coffee, picked up the cuppa and returned to the car to drink it because it was getting a little chilly.

We were simply sitting in the car, facing the local oval and chatting about my workout, his workday and making small talk. Then before I knew it I found myself kissing him.

I didn't push him away as I was enjoying the kiss. One thing led to the other and before we knew it we were in the back seat of the car – my pants were down around my ankles and his pants were down around his knees. The experience was unexpected. I was excited and so was he. We enjoyed our time together.

We chatted for a moment to reflect on what we just did and why we did it, aiming to make sense of it all. I knew that I liked him, but I hadn't imagined having a sexual encounter with him.

Anyway, I guess I was flattered that he took an interest in me in that way and thought nothing more of it. We got dressed. We both said some nice words to each other and that night ended.

I offered to take him home, but Michael asked if I could drop him off at a corner street and he would be okay to walk home from there. So I did.

I got home that evening, took my belongings out of the car and had a shower before going to bed. I knew that on the following day I had lectures to attend at Victoria University and had to get organised in the morning for that. That evening, I was tired, especially after all that I had just experienced, and crashed.

The following morning, I got out of bed, had another shower and ate my breakfast that was made for me by my father – that was kind of a routine in our household. Anyone who awoke early would begin to make breakfast for anyone else who was waking up. After breakfast I checked all the books that I had to take with me for that day, organised my swimming items for that evening, reached for my handbag to grab my car keys – and noticed my purse was missing.

I thought that was odd as I knew my purse was in my bag after swimming last night, even after the outing with Michael. Then it occurred to me that Michael must have stolen it, as he was the last person in my car and he would've had access to it.

I felt deceived and so stupid. Although, I wasn't that stupid, as I remembered Michael advising me what school he went to. So I rang up the school and asked to speak with him. I knew his surname so that was going to be an easy find. I just had to convince the school that I was doing a project for university and we were interviewing young men – a white lie that would allow me to speak with him. Security wasn't as tight in schools in the early 90s; you could get away with doing such things.

I got hold of Michael and of course he was very surprised that I was able to track him down. I confronted him with what he did and he admitted to it. He suggested to pick it up from his place directly after school and he would be there to give it back.

He provided his address details and so I went, alone. Another big mistake.

It was 4.30 pm that afternoon. My gut had bad vibes about this rendezvous, but I was being brave and knew that I had to get my purse back as it had all my bankcards and driver's licence – and a small amount of money, which wasn't going to be a focus in aiming to get back as I knew I was going to have to cut my losses and simply aim to get the purse back. Go into his house, get it and get out, hoping to never have anything to do with him again.

I arrived at the scene. I parked the car. I looked around to see if there was anyone else in the home and couldn't hear any noises. I walked up to the front door. It was a white-planked house, run-down, sloping and looking as if it was going to fall apart. I knew at this point that this experience simply just didn't feel right, yet I had to go through with it in order to break away and have nothing further to do with this guy. I knocked on the door; it was ajar. I heard Michael's voice from inside: 'Yeah come in, go straight down the hallway and I'm at the back.'

I thought, 'Shit, I now have to walk further into the home,' which was exactly what I didn't want to be doing. I was hoping he could come to the front door, give me my purse and I would get out of there as fast as I could.

I entered the home. I walked down the corridor as Michael had suggested. The house wasn't too bad. It did have a bad smell to it, like rotten bananas. Beds were unmade. Dirty dishes were left in the sink. As I walked down the corridor, he called out and said, 'I'm in here.'

'Here' was in a bedroom. My heart was pounding. I was feeling unwell in the stomach and I began to feel anxious. He pulled the door open, forcefully grabbed my hand, said, 'Here is your purse,' and handed it to me. I immediately placed it into my zipped bag. Then I'd hoped to depart, until I noticed he was still holding onto my hand. He pushed me onto the double-sized queen bed and said, 'You're not going anywhere.'

I said, 'Stop! Get off!' I shook my head from side to side while restricted and strapped by both his hands holding my hands down over my head. I couldn't move. I knew at this point I was in trouble. I aimed to lift my legs up and kick him, but the position I was forced into wasn't going to set me free at all.

At this point he forced himself onto me. He pushed his penis right up against my face and forced me to suck on it. All I wanted to do was get out of there as I was feeling extremely threatened for my life. I couldn't move. I completely shut down and froze. He then grabbed my pants and pushed them down towards my thighs. I was in serious trouble. I realised that if I was to aim to break free, that now was a possibility of hope. I would again aim to kick him in the groin.

I somehow managed to stumble onto my knees, and got up with my pants down around my ankles. He then grabbed hold of me once again and he forced his penis into my vagina from behind, not quite anal sex. It was at this point I was able to break free. He aimed to push his body harder up against mine. I reached down onto the floor and grabbed my bag, running out of the bedroom with my underwear around my ankles, attempting to get out of the house as fast as I could. I didn't even bother looking back.

I made it through the front door as it was still ajar. I quickly unlocked the car with my remote key. I threw my bag into the car, noticed my purse fall onto the floor in front of the passenger seat, started the car and drove away as fast as I could. Literally putting the pedal to the metal. I was too frightened to look back to see what he was doing. I was in complete shock with what I had just experienced. I came to realise I was assaulted and had officially become another statistic, a female victim of rape at only seventeen years of age.

I was in complete shame. I was embarrassed. I was mortified

and I promised myself that I would not tell a soul for as long as I live.

Unfortunately, as weeks went by I began feeling nauseous. I had put on weight. I had restless sleeps. I thought it was just from trying to deal with exams for university as I often ate late, had many late nights up studying and would eat high protein and fatty meals at odd hours through the day. I was also feeling extremely tired.

I booked myself in to see the local GP. I explained all my symptoms. I didn't say a word about my experiences with Michael. The doctor requested that I have urine and blood tests done to rule out all viral possibilities and immune system issues that may be brewing up. He also was concerned about my iron levels as they were low.

He came back and congratulated me. I asked, 'What for?'

He said, 'You're pregnant.'

The world just flashed by me right there and then. Once again I was in complete shock. I didn't know whether to smile and pretend to be happy or tell them that I cannot be pregnant. This could have happened because of me being raped.

The complexity of the circumstances thickens even more. I was also regularly seeing an older man at the time the rape happened; I now found myself wondering whose baby this was.

What was I to do? I didn't want to tell a soul. I would be kicked out of home. I would bring shame to my family, especially from the cultural background that I come from. My parents would simply disown me. My sisters would continuously call me a slut or something to that effect.

I didn't have any friends I could trust enough to tell them what had happened to me. I thought about ending my life, although I knew this wasn't a solution because I once had the thought of doing that when I was seventeen (for different reasons which I will share with you later on).

Once I knew I was pregnant, I began to ask why this had happened to me. How stupid of me. What have I done to my life? What outcomes will I have now? What success am I going to be? How am I going to continue going to university with a baby growing in my stomach? I knew that I couldn't have this baby. I wouldn't love it. I shouldn't even be having sex with men, how was I to explain all this? Where could I go to for help?

Remember that this was in the late 90s and they didn't have as many community services available as they do today, offering great service support in these areas.

I had to create another lie, but this time I had to tell the older man that I was pregnant with his baby. He would know what to do and he would help me get rid of it. Abort it, I should say. When I was seventeen, I can remember referring to it in this manner. All the learning and understanding that I have gained since then would have allowed me to express and refer to the circumstances differently.

So, I had to bring myself to tell this man that I was pregnant with his baby. I had met up with the secret lover, who I was only dating to abuse his services and connections to allow me to become successful. Such a stupid and naive thing to do. What was I thinking? Obviously I was a little selfish and wanted so desperately to become somebody important – I would've done anything at the age of seventeen.

I had planned the time I was going to tell him. I remember lying next to him in bed after having sex with him. He did say I was quieter than usual that afternoon. I would ask ad hoc questions: Would we ever get married? If we were married would you want children? If you had children would you accept them? He was twenty years older than me and had substantial credentials; he was able to put things into perspective for his own selfish needs.

Seriously, what was I thinking? As I write this story for the first time, knowing all that I know now, I think that if I only I had the education, the knowledge, the skills and the understanding – and more importantly, the maturity – to know then what I know now. My life would've been different for sure, and it would've led to other pathways and opportunities.

So without beating further around the bush, I told him. I said, 'I am pregnant.' He immediately replied, 'Well, how did that happen?' because we knew we were being very careful and using protection.

This man was high profile at the time; he would travel a lot and spend time with me when he was in Melbourne. I fitted into his glove cleverly and this relationship went on for three years. I did grow to think I cared for him a lot but I never loved him. I knew that my intention for having this relationship was purely for financial gain and success leading into my career, whatever that was going to be.

He was once married to a high school teacher, and he divorced her. I met her a few times and we became mild social friends. Weird relationship, although she didn't know that I was dating her ex-husband at the time. He had a young daughter who was eight years of age, therefore a single father. Was I to become a step-mum to this young girl who was half my age, if things got to the next level? What was I thinking? Crazy lifestyle.

I would get excited when he would call me to go out to prestigious events. I would lie to my parents and family and say that I was supporting him on these outings for work placement and I'd be getting paid for my time. Well, to some degree I was getting paid sexually but that was about it.

Thinking back, I actually didn't enjoy the sexual encounters. I can recall only ever having once experienced an orgasm during sex with him. All the other times he would get off quicker and the session would end very quickly.

I remember the first time he put his hand on me and being so nervous, again thinking to myself this was not the right thing to be doing. He knew what he was doing. He took advantage of my body and by me connecting with him in this way, it would allow him to regain his youthfulness and power over me. How stupid and naive I was.

I paid the price for this relationship as well. He too took advantage of my body and physically raped me. You think I would've learnt the first time – nope, I had to experience rape twice to really understand relationships and how people would take advantage of my kindness and gullibility.

What was wrong with me? Why did I crave success so badly? Why was it important for me to succeed?

Getting back to the abortion. He told me that we couldn't keep it. He was certain that it was our child because as far as he knew, he was the only man in my life. He supported me by paying for the abortion. He drove me down to the abortion clinic in Melbourne. He dropped me off there and drove off. That was his support …

I walked up a flight of stairs and pushed open the heavy reddish wooden door. I felt ready to throw up. I remember feeling light on my feet, knowing full well that I was about to terminate a life that had been growing inside of me. I sat there, waiting for someone to attend to me at the reception window. A young lady who appeared out of nowhere asked if she could help me. I replied, 'Yes, I am here because I have to terminate this pregnancy.'

I was then asked to fill in some paperwork and was handed a clipboard with a pen attached, and I filled in the sheet promptly. I walked back up to the window of the reception area and handed back the clipboard, pen and completed sheet. I then remember returning to my seat and as I sat there waiting, I began to ask myself, 'What the fuck am I doing here?' Although, I already knew the answer to that literal question. I think a better question was how I ended up there, and what was going to happen to me.

Just then I noticed another young girl lying on the bed being wheeled out into the foyer area, which was the room next door to the reception centre. I immediately said to myself, 'That is obviously where I'm going to go when they've finished with me, too.'

The lady called out my name. I acknowledged her and then she said, 'Come this way.' I kept saying to myself, 'Fuck, fuck, fuck. I'm scared. If there is a God help me, please … I'm sorry for what I am about to do.'

I was asked to wear a white gown and to take the bottom half of my clothes off. I didn't have any personal belongings with me, only my clothes. I laid down on the bed and was given an injection. I found myself talking to some surgeons, two men, wearing green protection guards over their mouths. I remember telling them a story about me, and before I knew it, I was off asleep. Obviously a general anaesthetic was administered for them to do what they had to do to remove and abort the baby.

The next thing I can recall is waking up and opening my eyes slowly. I was really drowsy. I was advised that everything was all over and I was free to go when ready. That was the end of that. As soon as I was able, I got dressed and walked out of there with complete regret and sadness in my heart. This was an overburdening weight and pain in my soul that I could never explain or tell anyone about.

The man who dropped me off picked me up. I didn't say a word. He said, 'All done and over with now.' Almost a sense of relief for him, even though I knew that it wasn't his child to begin with. I fell asleep in the car. I woke up again when we arrived at his unit. I fell asleep for a little bit longer and when I awoke this time I was in the rental apartment on my own. I figured he had gone off on another business trip or wherever, and now it was my time to leave as well.

I was fit enough to drive back home and went straight into my bedroom. That evening I had very little to say and simply pretended like it was another day at university.

I knew I had to let it go and continue to pretend that it never happened. I had to block the entire event out of my head, forever. No one was ever to find out, even though I knew exactly what had happened.

*

A few years later, I successfully graduated and received my Bachelor of Arts, majoring in communication studies and policy studies and sub-majoring in journalism. I successfully completed this degree in 1994.

That was also the year that my second rape occurred. It wasn't as violent as the first experience, but I was violated physically and battered emotionally.

The relationship with the older man continued for almost four years. I decided it had to end. I'd just ended a short relationship with another young man my age and I thought it was unfair that I should be playing around with another man while still engaging in sexual activities with this older man.

The older man was potentially having other flings anyway. I figured out over time that he already was engaging in sexual activities with other young women – providing false hopes for them as well.

So I decided to see him at his Melbourne offices one afternoon. It was a 3.00 pm appointment. I remember having trouble finding car parking spots available where I wouldn't have to pay for the spot that I was in, as I wasn't planning on staying for too long.

I had it all worked out in my head. Two days prior, I knew that he would be back in Melbourne from his business trips and I left a long letter under the front door at his rental apartment, ending the relationship with him. I requested to terminate whatever it was that we had. Don't get me wrong – I cared for him, yet he was old enough to be my father. He wasn't giving me what I really wanted, even though I thought what I wanted was to become successful while hanging out with this guy, meeting and greeting his networks and having the opportunity to prove myself to others how good an employee I was.

I guess I was hoping to be noticed, to be worthy of all that I could offer as a person. Now I understand that I allowed my body to become the vehicle for my success with men, my career and my finances – how naive was I.

I'd hoped he would accept the explanation and let it go. Unfortunately, he didn't like the idea of me ending the relationship with a letter. I believe it is because he wasn't in control of the conversation – I was.

I finally found a parking spot under a nice shady tree. I ensured that I didn't have to place money in the meter. I took nothing in my hands. I placed my handbag in the boot of my car. I locked the car and began to walk towards the big old historical building.

I recall feeling really nervous once again. I was sick in my stomach. I kept telling my inner voice that this would be quick. I'd stick to what I had already written and not deviate from what was advised and end the relationship. Whatever questions he may have, I would answer them honestly and that will be that.

Well, I knocked on his office door. He called out, 'Come in

and sit down.' It was a huge room, almost two rooms in one. A long brown desk and huge overarched armchairs to sit in.

I then said, 'Okay, so I guess you've read the letter I left for you?'

He said, 'Yes, and I must say I'm surprised that you would want to end the relationship for another man.'

He immediately wanted to probe me about this other man. I said, 'Well, let's face it, I am still very young. And yes, he is closer to my age – we have a few other things in common and that we can relate to.'

So he preceded to ask, 'Have you only just met him or have you known him for a while?'

I replied, 'No, I have known him for a while.'

The conversation was awkward and I had no idea why he really wanted to know so much. He then said, 'Well okay, if this is what you want. We can't have anything more to do with each other.'

I said, 'We could still be friends.'

He said, 'No, I don't think we can.' At this point he got up out of his chair, walked towards me and requested a final hug.

I was feeling a little uncomfortable about the idea and thought, 'Well, what is a final hug? It's really not that big of deal.' I was conversing with my inner voice and we agreed to give him a final hug before getting out of there as quickly as I could, once again, never to look back.

That final hug was the mistake I made. I wasn't strong enough to say no. I wasn't strong enough to pull away either. He grabbed hold of me and lured me to the ground. Unzipping his pants, he pulled out his penis and restrained me. I asked him to stop and that we shouldn't end this way. He didn't say anything and just went for it with pure lust on his behalf.

Once again, I froze, I didn't say a word. I tried to wriggle my way out from under him, but I was pressed so hard against the floor I could smell the dust in the carpet as I continued to swing my head from side to side. He kissed me all over and held me so tight that I just couldn't move.

He finished jerking off on me. Got up. Cleaned himself up. I remained on the floor shocked as he said, 'Well, you can go now!'

I bolted out of there thinking once again, 'What the fuck just happened?' I was trying to control the shock of it all. I was just assaulted by this man. Was I to tell anyone? I saw a security guard up ahead as I stormed out of the office – for a moment I was about to tell all, but I couldn't. I couldn't say a word. I was in shock and I was afraid. He had power and a profile in the public eye. I couldn't say a word to anyone.

I got back to my car, opened up my car boot, took my bag out, opened up the driver's door and drove off in tears. Pouring my eyes out, crying like a whale would call out for its mother. Speaking out aloud and saying how stupid and naive I was. 'What the fuck just happened to me', I asked myself once again.

To be honest, I blocked out everything that happened after that moment in my memory. Although I now know the memory was stored in my subconscious mind; in 2015, when I had undergone hypnotherapy, the memory of the experience came back on a conscious level, and I wasn't expecting it to at the time. This is why I believe we must reveal all that happens, good and bad, to allow the mind to be at ease. Forgiveness was given but I can never forget the act.

I heard about his later movements and kept my distance, really trying hard to never have anything to do with him again. He called me up once and advised that he was in Melbourne, wanting to catch up for a coffee as if nothing had ever happened. I immediately made up an excuse and said no. Yet I felt compelled to tell him what I was doing in my life at the time. I shared information about my family, my husband and my children. I didn't want to say anything, I just felt that he had this control over me and that I didn't have the courage to say, 'None of your business, fuck off,' because that is really what I wanted to say back then. The conversation was short, thank God for that.

Later in 1994, I successfully gained work in my dream job in film and television. I remember clearly having the interview with a young man; he had soft, curly light brown hair, had recently married and was one of the production managers for human resources, with the authority to hire and fire people. I remember this young man being very sceptical in hiring me, not because he hadn't believed my skills and credentials but because he was hiring someone via a different stream system of hiring, dealing with me directly.

I actually can't recall exactly how the arrangement for the interview was set up, but I do remember putting myself out there and talking to anyone and everyone who was able to give me a job. I was desperate and proactive in my younger days, aiming for success and knowing that I could land any job I wanted because I believed in my dream.

Further to meeting with this young man, he then introduced me to an older man named 'Bobbie Works'. He would've been in his late 40s, maybe even early 50s. His capacity of hiring was on different terms completely. This is where I discovered that politics and sexual favours could work for you if you were willing to do that, in order to make progress in the industry. Yes, I am talking about being taken advantage of in return for job placements in positions of some importance.

At this point, I had to make decisions. Was I going to allow my body to be used and abused, offering sexual favours to the big boss in order to get ahead in my career? I thought about his proposition for weeks. Knowing that he would often ask me out on private dinner dates to discuss my job prospects and possibilities, simply to take advantage of my body in return, didn't sit right with my gut.

I couldn't do it. It would be wrong for me to bring myself down, to devalue me. To pretend to be something that I am not. To be used and abused and exploited for sexual favours in return for career advancements. I refused every offer he requested and that clearly proved I would never get where I wanted to go because I didn't give him what he wanted. I wasn't going to be controlled by a man this way ever again.

This, of course, played a big role on my job outcomes and opportunities. As an employee at the time I had the opportunity to apply for other positions and all were turned down. Before I knew it, my contract ended. Strings were pulled to boot me out. One manager would talk to another manager, then another and so on. I had others in the workplace who believed in me and supported all the skills and abilities that I could clearly apply to many jobs, yet it wouldn't have mattered. No matter who I spoke to, how hard I tried, I didn't have the mental stamina and knowledge to put a case forward and expose what was truly going on behind the scenes. Once again I was afraid of what people would think and how ridiculous I would look.

When I was let go, I felt like my life was yet again over. I felt like I had made the wrong decisions. I remember driving down to the beach that afternoon after the last day of employment and sitting on the sand for hours, crying my heart out, watching the ripples in the ocean as the tide came in and sunset was commencing. I remember having conversations with my inner ego and asking myself, 'Why didn't I just sleep with the old man? If I had given him what he wanted, I would've had what I wanted and I would still be in a job.'

Then, I stopped. I asked the same questions over and over in my head, until everything played in slow motion in front of me. All I could hear was the sea. I could feel the wind blowing gently, landing on my face and down the side of my arms. I could also feel the heat from the sand as I buried my bare feet in it. I had a moment when I thought I could hear another voice, feel another presence and see other visions in the distance.

I wasn't sure if I was hallucinating or not. Was I dehydrated and perhaps hadn't drank enough water, releasing so much of it in tear form that I had no water left in my body? Very unlikely, but was it at all possible?

As I looked up into the sunset, I could hear someone saying, 'Hey, it's okay. Pick yourself up and keep going. You are not alone, it is not the end of the world and you can grow. Let it go and move on.' Was this God talking to me?

At this point, I found myself taking in a deep breath. I said to myself, 'It's going to be okay. Why would I want to sleep with a man just for a job? I don't need to do this nor should I be feeling guilty about this. This is not something that I should even contemplate. What the fuck was I thinking?'

Okay. I stopped again. I wiped the tears away. I felt the sand in between my fingers and pushed myself up off the sandy beach. I approached the water and said, 'Time to let go and move on.' I didn't know it at the time but I had entered into fellowship with Christianity; I could say that this was a 'kyros moment' and that I had re-blessed myself with the holy water of the seas to begin my new career journey. I do believe now that it was God speaking and reaching out to me.

I returned back to the spot where I left my shoes and looked around to see if there was anybody else in sight – not a soul around, only mine and me alone. I took a deep breath and continued to walk for ages. I finally returned to my car and drove home.

When I arrived home, I told my parents that my contract had

ceased and that there wasn't any other employment available for me to pursue – therefore, it was time for me to let go and move on.

My health was also under threat at the time; I was instructed by doctors that I had to change careers or the television industry would be the death of me. Having such a passion for my work, I committed to working all sorts of ridiculous hours, running around all over the place with very little sleep. This type of work practice was not sustainable and eventually it caught up with me. Although, it was my passion and I still have a love for it today.

That is when I thought, 'Well, what am I going to do and where am I going to be working?' This is when I pursued a career with Telstra, where I was successfully employed full-time. I travelled from Broadmeadows into the city on public transport for six years.

This is where new beginnings were to commence in my career.

# Awareness of Spiritual Senses

I remember being at primary school in the early 80s. At one point I changed from Meadow Heights Primary School, based in Broadmeadows, to Preston West Primary School. This was my parents' decision, as my late mother picked up work in West Preston in a factory and both my older siblings were enrolled in the high school, not far from the primary school that I was to attend. Therefore, it made sense for Mum to have all children attending schools close to each other and not far from her workplace. This would make it manageable for her to do pick-ups and drop-offs, from home to school and work and vice versa.

At Meadow Heights, a school building that no longer exists today (it was taken over and refurbished over the years, eventually changing into an Islamic college) provided me with some foundations in my early learning and development.

Unfortunately, my memories of early learning are not of any academic standards but profound emotional developments.

My education influenced my perception of trust in people and self-esteem. It had an impact on what and how I felt about events that occurred. My experiences caused me to feel a little distant from others and a little withdrawn.

I recall specifically a time when I had nits, in prep. My mother had shaved my head, leaving me bald and going to school with a bright yellow French beret. I asked my mother if it would be okay that I didn't go to school until my hair grew back.

Mum thought that was a ridiculous idea; I would go to school and everything would be fine. Nobody would notice if I had hair or not.

Well, throughout that early morning nobody did notice that I hadn't hair on my head, until all the children were asked to sit on the mat, as the teacher was getting all the students in the class organised and preparing us for show 'n' tell, that early morning on the second day of my school life.

I remember just as we all sat down, a young girl sitting directly behind me had to serve her curiosity as she pulled the beret off my head, causing my head to be exposed to all the class. As a result, everyone looked and laughed directly at me.

Of course I was in shock; I was trying to get my beret back from the girl who'd pulled it off, as she was waving it around in the air so I wouldn't be able to reach it. Evidently, I created enough noise for the teacher to notice me and to bring to her attention that something terrible had just happened to me, so that she aimed to stop the chaos for me, quickly.

I simply froze and cried.

I don't remember the girl's name or my teacher's name, I just remember being humiliated and embarrassed. I had now had become a key focus to the class and everyone else who may have been in the room at the time.

The teacher decided to allow me the opportunity to share my story, as to why I didn't have any hair. Imagine that. A prep student wanting to sit in class and be invisible for a day or two becomes the focus for opening discussion for all the students to learn about why I didn't have any hair on my head.

Great. I didn't know about nits. I only knew I had these little bugs crawling in my hair and Mum immediately shaved my head, leaving me hairless.

The teacher explained what nits were, why we got them, how we get them and why it was important to tie hair back in a bun, especially if you had long hair.

It was a great learning session with loads of information to take in, but I was disappointed and embarrassed – once again, I had to be the subject of exploration and explanation.

As I reflect back on this now, as an adult, I could agree that if a student hadn't had nits, every one of us in that class might've never learnt about them and how to prevent having lice ever again. My situation provided all the students of that class in that room a very insightful learning session. That would be the grown up teacher explanation and putting a positive spin on the traumatic outcome that I had experienced at such a young age.

However, as a counsellor and a coach, if I was to dive in a little further and analyse how this experience affected my emotional state, it would've been a trigger and could've become a hindrance to my self-esteem and confidence. Lucky for me, I guess – I must have had excellent support in place at school for me to be able to attend school the following week, as I clearly remember this happening on a Friday. I had the weekend to grow an inch of hair before Monday came around.

As years went on and I transferred into Grade 5 at Preston West Primary School, my favourite educative learnings were

Art, Religious Instruction and Maths. I liked drawing, painting and being involved in all facets of creating and making different artworks.

I had an interest in religion. The subject was foreign to me and I was curious to see how I could connect with it and make sense of what I was exposed to at home and how it was different to what I was exposed to at school. For example, watching my mother walk around the house, room to room, blessing and chanting each room as she entered it, waving around a gold goblet filled with light charcoal blocks smoking the house out every Sunday, along with attending the Greek Orthodox Church in Fawkner, St Niktarios, on significant celebrations like Easter, christenings, weddings and sometimes Christmas.

My mother never explained any of the proceedings that she would do in detail, only to suggest that by blessing the house, she was keeping the evil spirits away and allowing the Holy Spirit within our home. For each of us, this meant that we were all blessed and covered with this Holy Spirit as each room was being blessed.

I have come to understand that this is a practice that Orthodox Christians undertake as part of a ritual that goes back generations. It is a belief highly valued in people's homes today, but only for those who want to accept that there is a spiritual presence in our universe can this spiritual ritual have an impact on our lives.

I personally had encountered many of what I now have come to understand as 'kyros' moments. I didn't understand them back in my younger days but I have come to understand them today. Moments where I had felt and seen Jesus during meditation and workshop were my kyros moments. Times when I asked for God's help were my kyros moments. Moments that healed my soul, allowing me to feel passion and trust in myself and for others again by developing this intimate relationship with God, were and continue to be my kyros moments.

My first ever experience with understanding who Jesus was and what he was truly about was when I felt Him and His presence in my heart. I recall listening to a radio program holding an appeal, aiming to raise $542,000 to keep the community station on air. They already had over 800,000 active and potential listeners as stated on their website. The station offered rich and valuable programs and effective sponsorship announcements meaningful to members of the community.

Each person would ring through to the radio station, dial the number, and once on air they would have the opportunity to share a story on how the radio station has supported them, or their family or a friend, to get through another day of living.

Every story was heartfelt and certainly resonated with other people in society; most were associated with some level of painful experience. This one particular story came on air and it was named 'George's Story'. It was based on George's experiences and hardship. His wife was experiencing chemotherapy after being diagnosed over a course of three years with cancer symptoms, being fortunate with therapy to eradicate the disease once and for all. Along with dealing with hospital visitations regularly, George also had to attend to his children and his unwell mother, and deal with the loss of his father. His wife had experienced a car accident, and he was relying on his car that could only just make it from point A to point B. He had no hot water in his home, leaving him and his children to bathe in cold water, waiting patiently for boiled water to be available to pour into the cold bathtub for some form of warmth while washing up.

George was unemployed and offered his last $100 to the station because he had been listening to the station time and time again to get him through the difficult encounters that he had experienced. George wasn't a religious man, yet he knew that he had to provide to the station and donate what he had available, despite of all the hardships and personal experiences that he hesitantly shared on air with 800,000 potential listeners – me being one of them.

I found myself pulling over on the side of the highway. I called the radio station and requested that I donate $100 to George and his family directly. After hearing George's story, my heart was pounding and hurting for him.

I believe at that very moment God was speaking through me. Even though I too was doing it tough financially, with my husband not working at the time and me having transitioned from full-time teaching into part-time for only two days. We had a $200,000 mortgage to pay off on our home, along with school fees and household bills. I was thinking that I was not the best person to provide funds to this person, but I knew I had to do it because it's what people do in time of need. We should be giving, sharing, offering and supporting others more than ourselves.

As I pulled over, flooded tears in my eyes, on hold to the radio station as they were confirming if it was okay to accept my funds and provide it directly to George and his family, I looked up to watch the cars driving by on the highway – only to see the pastor's car driving by that very minute. I said out aloud, 'God, if this is not confirmation of a sign, I honestly don't know what is.'

Fortunately, the volunteer that I was chatting with on the line enthusiastically advised that they were able to process my request and the funds would go directly to George's family.

I was so happy. That very moment I knew that God was pleased with me. My heart was filled with unconditional love for myself and for someone I have never met.

The following weekend during Sunday church and worshipping,

I prayed and thanked God for his delivery to me and how I knew for certain it was Him. Once again during my prayer time and meditative state, I had a vision and felt His presence within me.

I felt full of unconditional love. It's so difficult to explain the feeling unless you experience it yourself and believe that it can happen to you. I often talked to others about my experiences and everyone had a different view and opinion.

I knew what was real. I knew what I felt and continue to feel. I now know that God is with me. I have come to understand when we choose to see, feel and hear the things that we want mostly in our lives, our own realities are altered and changes occur that become significant milestones in our lives. These changes appear to be coincidental and yet I ask, are they? The path that we experience goes off to a different road and begins to present itself differently, with a new map forming, a new beginning for better outcomes.

Since that day, I have come to understand that having knowledge about religion and believing in religion are in fact two different forms of understanding. When you truly begin to feel, it's like you are on a high – it would be like taking drugs or smoking marijuana. Once, in Year 12 on muck up day, I smoked a bong for the first time; I became light-headed and I was feeling so relaxed. I tried it once and once was enough. Drug smoking wasn't for me. But in regards to belief, the body and mind sensation you receive can feel similar to that.

The love that I have for the Lord that I have never met, yet have seen in my visions, is truly miraculous. Events like this follow me, and will continue to follow and grow in me.

I understand that God is great. That He can provide all things for us when we enter into a relationship with Him. When we believe and feel His presence in our hearts, only then can you truly see changes that are real and of benefit to yourself.

You also understand how one can become a better version of themselves.

I know this now because of what I once experienced on the beach, moving away safely from the two accounts of rape, and answering me when I thought about suicide. In response to all of these incidences, I truly believe that I felt God's presence within my soul; he had given me a 'sign' for a new direction, keeping me safe when my thoughts and experiences were once out of my control.

During one of the church's worship sessions and while I was praying, I remember asking the Lord to provide me with the wisdom and strength needed to succeed and support our local community, with new victories and better outcomes for the residential members of our community. For better implementations of infrastructure, for growth in employment, for support in small local businesses and so forth. As I had been approached to run for local council, I thought it best to pray for it first and see, hear or feel something towards this vision and if it was a path for me to follow.

During this procession, miraculously, I felt the shakes as if I was having a seizure; I felt God's warmth and the heat of my palms in my hands. I felt Him and that feeling was absolutely beautiful. It left me speechless, as it was truly a unique experience and it was so grand and overwhelming.

This is why I believe in God. This is why I like to encourage others to feel, see or hear Him as I have experienced to date. The moments are short, sharp and shiny, but boy they powerful and worth it. Every breath I take in God's presence is worth a thousand lives and worth living to experience.

The interesting aspect of all of this is that I haven't had any formal training in religion; it is what I have chosen to expose myself to and learn. It is via discussion, some Bible studies and the catechism that I expose myself to, as well as hanging around like-minded people, in understanding more about

God and what He wants us, his children, to build in reflection of Him within our souls. It's a life of supporting, giving, sharing, providing and being present in the moment for others, each and every day. In return, receiving and delivering true salvation and being free from sin and difficulties in our lives.

Amen to God. God is great and believing in Him is truly a life of abundance in all areas of life. We are all on this journey, in our mortal state, and through God we experience our own eternities and appreciate the life that we have been blessed with.

# High School Motives and Emotives

I remember having a high school sweetheart. A young Italian boy named Frank Guriato. He came from a traditional Italian family. He had beliefs and values about Greek and Italian culture. He was really keen to go out with me and I even remember the time he asked me out.

We were in various classes together in Year 10. It was the end of the Psychology session that I was taking and he had just completed Maths. He said, 'I want to ask you something.'

I replied, 'Sure, go ahead.'

He said, 'I really like you. I think you're smart, beautiful and I want you to go out with me, so would you be my girlfriend?'

Just like that. I was gobsmacked. He knew, like most people knew at school including the teachers, that I was extremely career-driven and would not allow anything or anyone stand in my way of my success. As a student heading into Year 11 I knew that I had a hard year to come and I wanted to focus on my studies.

I replied, 'I will think about it and let you know tomorrow.' He left it at that, said goodbye and that was the end of that conversation.

I had my school bag and books on my back, ready to walk towards the back of the school where I was to meet my sisters before walking to the bus stop. The whole way down I was chatting with my best friend Sandy Goodwill, who I still have contact with today. She said, 'Well, what are you going to tell him? I reckon you should, he's a nice boy and he would respect you.'

I said, 'Yeah, I know – that's the problem. He is a nice boy. What if he's the one that ruins my career ambitions, plans and directions?'

Cindy said, 'What are you talking about? You've got plenty of time before that even happens. Who knows, things might go really well... and you may end up marrying him. Just tell him yes and be done with it.'

That evening, when we said our goodbyes, I couldn't stop thinking about his proposal and the way he was a real gentleman when he asked me to go out with him. As a tall, clever European girl, born in Australia and wearing glasses, I didn't think I was attractive enough for any man to like me for who I am and not just want sex out of me or use me for anything.

I thought he was a sweet young man who was genuine about his offer and really did like me. I knew it because I felt his heart pounding from a distance, that afternoon when he asked me, but I didn't tell him that.

All night I couldn't sleep. Frank was on my mind. I knew that I too liked him and that he would treat me right and respectfully. So I awoke the next morning, caught the bus and got off at the standard bus stop, ready to walk to school – and Frank was standing up near the green-grassed hill that was located upon entering Preston Technical School (as it was once known, before it changed its name to Preston Secondary College).

He walked up towards me and I could feel my heart racing. I knew that he was keen to have an answer and wanted to know where he stood. I said, 'Good morning,' and he replied by saying good morning back. I asked him how he slept and he advised how he didn't get much sleep at all because he was thinking about me and really keen to know my answer. I said to him that I was the same, and that I didn't sleep much either because I was thinking about my response. I let him know that my answer was yes, and that I would be happy to be his girl.

Just then Frank grabbed my hand, gave me the biggest hug in the world and pecked me on the lips. It was exciting times for us young lovebirds.

Our relationship came to be known by everyone over the three years that we were together. The teachers were aware of our relationship – some friends of mine and other parents knew of it as well. Some of my own family members also knew. However, as time went on during the three years together, more and more people did became aware – and that included our parents.

We did our best for a long time to not tell my parents about our relationship because we were fearful of what they would say. We knew they wouldn't have approved of our relationship, therefore we did our best to keep it from them. Our families were traditional, so both sides would've encouraged marriage, which is not what Frank and I would've wanted.

I recall going to my first ever school camp in Year 12. My parents only allowed me to go to camp because it was mandatory, otherwise they wouldn't have contemplated the idea of letting me go at all.

The camp was based in Anglesea, Melbourne, and we were to camp out in cabins close to the beach. We were going to learn socialisation and team building skills and about dealing with friendships, sexual education and the like.

Frank and I had planned that this location was going to be where we were going to have our first sexual experience together. We were young adults, both about seventeen years of age, and knew that we wanted to be together. We were responsible and intended to use a condom during our sexual encounter. I planned it and discussed how it was going to happen and how we were going to manage it all, without getting caught by the teachers. In hindsight, we were brave to contemplate all that we did; obviously young lust and love for each other was the driving factor of so desperately wanting to be together and forever.

It was late and everyone, teacher and students alike, went to bed and stationed themselves in the cabins that we were all assigned to. The boys were separate to the girls. Frank came to my cabin when he felt it was safe to do so and all lights were out across the whole site. As he knocked on the door, I opened it. I was on the top bunk bed and my friend was on the bottom; she was sound asleep.

He quietly and gently climbed into bed with me. We had a discussion about whether we were absolutely sure that this was the right thing to do. Of course my sexual drive was in overload and I just wanted to go for it and experience it all. It wasn't what I imagined it to be, however – I was willing to do it with him because I truly believed in my heart that this young man was my soul mate and he would be with me no matter what – and vice versa, forever. Such naivety as a teenager.

So we kissed with great passion and our breathing was getting heavy, faster and louder. I took my underwear off under the covers and left them there so no one else would come to notice; he did the same. I guided Frank's penis into my vagina and we began to do it. As we were bouncing up and down on the top bunk of the bed, it began to creak and make sounds – I suggested that we be quieter and aim to slow it down. Frank was aiming to break my hymen and he had a lot of trouble doing so. We both were true virgins. We ensured that we placed the condom on correctly because we didn't want to be irresponsible and we wanted it to be 'right'.

Well, we didn't quite reach climax and we didn't finish what we started. We both agreed that we would stop and we would try again some other time when it was suitable and better planned, with perhaps a better bed arrangement.

Frank pulled out from inside of me. He searched for his underwear in the bed and slid them back on. He zipped up his jeans and quietly left the cabin, being extremely careful that he didn't get caught coming out of our cabin. A bright light was on in the distance where the shared toilets were located. He went there pretending that he needed to go to the toilet. I followed him afterwards, and noticed him leaving the toilets from the distance. What an experience and memory that was.

After that incident, I attempted to go back to sleep and found it difficult to do so. Morning came before we knew it – we all got up out of bed, got dressed and went to the kitchen for our team duties.

*

I recall one day when my father had picked me up from school because my mother couldn't make it and he found me sitting next to Frank; we were holding hands on a hilltop park site that was part of our school complex. It was the end of the day. Frank left me there to deal with my father, and so I did.

Of course, like any parent my father wasn't impressed and he was in shock. He never thought that his little girl would have a relationship at school, as his visions and expectations of me were very high. He wanted me to be successful in my life and to be proud of my achievements. I could never do anything to deviate away from my schooling and education, like be involved in a relationship. I also could do no wrong in my father's eyes because he did value and believe in me and my dreams that I would constantly share with him. He was the one who would drive me to different locations in Melbourne, so I could experience what I truly believed I wanted in my life through extra-curricular activities that included attending drama classes, dancing and modelling schools.

I knew that there wasn't any way that my father would support and approve the circumstances that I was involved in, at that present time.

I guess he believed in me and wanted me to do more with my life than fall in love, get married, have children and be a house mum, which is what my sisters did. He only ever had the best intentions at heart for me and wanted me to succeed in something.

My father knew how hard it was to obtain an education and how his parents couldn't afford to send him to school – he became a fisherman from his own life experiences. Fishing daily, only to support his family and to provide food on the table each night for his parents and his siblings to eat.

I recall my father walking towards me on the hill, asking me a million and one questions, just like any parent would. I knew that I did wrong and that he was disappointed in me in a big way. I also knew that I was dishonest, and felt as if I had failed him.

We went to the office and I was signed out of school for the day. In the car, there was silence. Neither of us spoke to each other until we got home.

My father asked me what my intentions were with this boy. Before I even began to speak, he demanded that I end the relationship immediately and that unless we were prepared to get married, we were not to continue seeing each other as boyfriend and girlfriend. My father didn't insist that I couldn't see him again – he knew that was unlikely to happen, since we were at the same school and we were bound to see each other during class times. Although he did also advise that he would take me out of school and place me into another school if I didn't end the relationship.

I knew he was angry with me and disappointed in me. However, it wouldn't make sense that I change schools as I was close to completing Year 12. I know he suggested that out of anger and fear of not letting go and moving on with his demands. In some way he wanted to ensure that he still had control and influence with the decisions that he made for me, simply because he said so – enforcing his beliefs, values and personal experiences.

I demanded an explanation as to why I couldn't see Frank and continue having a relationship with him. He bluntly advised that we are to be reminded that school is where we go to get an education, and if I thought that I was learning while having a boyfriend than we were kidding ourselves. He stated the obvious about why it was important to go to school: to have some form of education behind us.

My older sisters didn't complete in school and did get married in their teens, and my father could see that their journey was different to mine. He strongly recommended that I didn't make the same choices as they did. Besides, I knew that when Dad spoke so seriously about a topic, with passion and meaning, there was no turning back or changing his mindset. Dad had spoken – it was very much a one way conversation and that was the end of that.

This was when I felt my life pass right by, before my very eyes. At least, that's where my thinking and mindset was at. I was at a loss.

Frank and I had been secretly going out behind my parents'

backs for some time. We knew that our good times had come to an end and as much as we didn't want to let go and move on, we had to because my father said so.

So the next morning, I had to be the bearer of bad news. I got to school that morning and saw Frank standing in the corridor close to the stairway. He had asked how things went last night with my father. I teared up and advised that he didn't approve of our relationship and that we had to end it. Today was going to be the last day of thinking that we were going to have a deep and meaningful relationship of any sort. We would not be connected, now and in the future.

What we had was deep – at least we thought it was, being our first time experiencing sex, foreplay and other romantic and lustful rendezvous. And it all came to an end.

I was devastated and so was he.

If only my father wasn't so strict, I thought – if only he could understand the significance and impact that Frank had in my life at that time. Unfortunately, he couldn't and chose not to entertain the idea by any means. Dad was a man of his word and when he stamped his foot down on an idea, you stuck to it. This was a part of being Greek I didn't enjoy about our culture – his strictness.

I was too scared to argue any further with my father, therefore I followed his instructions and felt at that time that my life was ruined. I wanted to disappear and thought of committing suicide by jumping off a bridge because of it.

I cried for days. I wasn't happy and I didn't have any motivational skills left in me to want to continue my future aspirations. I didn't want to go to school. I repeatedly told myself if I couldn't live a life with Frank, then what life would I be living?

I was a young girl who was popular at school with her peers and teachers, and yet I wanted to end my life. Until something inside me, an overwhelming emotion that took me by surprise, helped me get through it all. Over time I was able to let him go and move on.

That something inside me was once again God. I didn't know that at the time, yet I know it now.

I have come such a long way with my emotional state over the years. I live to be happy and follow my passion – and my journey was very different to what I had planned.

# Vipassana, Woori Yallock

In 2012, it was suggested by a dear friend, whom I have known for over twenty years, that I attend a Vipassana meditation centre in Woori Yallock to get away for a while.

After my mother's passing in May of 2012, I was no longer my usual self. I was diagnosed with post-traumatic stress disorder and mild depression. I felt it would be the ideal time for me to follow my friend's advice and book myself into this distant and rather foreign place to me.

I had a conversation with my family and advised them that I would be away for ten days. I would not be able to contact them and they would not be able to contact me, unless in extreme emergency. They supported my decision.

*

At the retreat in Woori Yallock, I had to become accustomed to following and committing to strict rules and regulations outlined by the centre.

I had to separate myself from the world that I was living in and experience a place where I would have an opportunity to truly relax, discover my inner thoughts and occupy a land of new opportunities and complete rejuvenations.

This place had set rules that had to be followed for a structured period of time. For ten nights and eleven days you were expected to live away from home, in a cabin with two other strangers. You were not allowed to make eye contact with anybody else on site. You were not allowed to speak with anyone else. You were not allowed to read, write or use any form of technology. All the things I have a passion about and that are dear to my heart were to be removed from my life for eleven days straight.

What we were committing to was regular wake-ups every day and without fail at 4.00 am. We were required to attend the meditation hall daily. The room was split into two large halves. Men were segregated to one side and the women on the other. Once the 'old lady' and her personal assistant were ready to proceed with their meditation, everyone had to get settled by sitting on the floor, on top of blue pillows and cushion supports. If you wanted to, you were able to sit on a chair, but only for short periods of time and you had to provide a medical reason as to why you could have that privilege.

Not a sound from anyone in the meditation hall. The video would begin on the big screen and we would all sit in silence, listening to the voice on the screen. Once this part concluded, then we were to watch the speaker on the screen explain concepts and what we may see, feel or hear during our time in the meditation hall.

Such solitude in one room and yet so many people doing exactly the same thing at the same time. Complete silence experienced by all of us, in our own minds and in the room, for one hour straight. Sometimes during processions we were advised that we could have a 5–10 minute break and that was only to go to the toilet and stretch a little.

For ten days straight this was the procedure that had to be fulfilled by all of us. We each agreed to do exactly that when we decided to stay after the first night of listening to an audio recording of the rules and regulations and completing the paperwork and consent forms.

The rooms would get very smelly and very warm with everyone's odours. You could hear any noise that was made, including the people who would accidentally pop off – that usually was the men, and sadly because nobody was allowed to speak, nobody excused themselves.

I was committed to my cause, even though I didn't know for certain what I had signed up for. I didn't know what to expect as each day came about.

I always looked forward to the food during lunchtime and breakfast; in the evenings you could only eat one piece of fruit, an apple or an orange.

At lunchtimes, however, the meals were divine. Nothing was ever made with meat; it was as if I'd also committed to a vegan diet. Everything I ate included vegetables, legumes, soups, bread and loads of variations of nuts. It was extremely healthy eating for the whole duration that I was there and the opportunity to experience a little detox, as we all cleansed our bodies with the food that was prepared for us daily.

I was pleased that the weather was brilliant. We had a couple of nights of rain and some land became a little bumpy, muddy, slippery and wet, but it was bearable.

I remember getting my period and knew that I had packed a few sanitary pads but that they weren't going to last – and that meant I had to communicate with the 'old lady's' assistant once again.

I imagine that she loved what she did and appeared to be a very merciful lady who obeyed all the rules and was obedient. Actually, now that I think about it and having learnt all that I have about faith today, I guess I can suggest that she was acting as a Christ-like character. She was very giving, sharing and helpful in times of need. I am so glad she came through with my pads as I was beginning to think that I would have to use toilet paper for the remainder of my time at Woori Yallock.

The first night on site was all about finding our way. Finding our cabins and settling in. We were to organise our beds and have them ready every night. We all found this part a little awkward as we weren't allowed to speak to each other or even look at each other. It was tricky when it came to sleep time as we left the light on until the last person would go to bed – only then could switch the lights off, signalling to all that it was time for all of us to go to sleep. It was as if I had told my own daughter, 'Lights out and time for bed.' That felt really weird. Of course I was a little wired up because I'd begun to think about what I have done.

I knew that it was going to be located in the middle of nowhere but hadn't been sure what to expect. Lucky I had my torch, and even that I aimed to keep hidden under my sleeping bag so the light wasn't bright enough for others in the cabin. A really weird experience.

Each time I could recall waiting to see who was to turn their light off first, knowing that each morning was going to be an early wake-up call for all of us.

At exactly 4 am every morning without fail, we heard the gongs going off. You would hear a long deep pitch radiating through the silence of the early morning and hear the sound fade out right through until the donging disappeared.

The first thing I would do was race for the toilet. I would quickly go back to my cabin and get dressed. Then I would return to the toilets, wash my face, brush my teeth and hair and then return to my cabin. I would place a warm cardigan or jumper over me, as the early mornings were fresh, and walked towards the meditation hall. We all would take off our shoes outside the hall and enter the hall silently, taking our places where we had decided to position our pillowcases and covers to begin meditation.

I had come to find sitting cross-legged on the floor was a little uncomfortable for me as I suffered from a herniated lower disc. Sometimes the disc would pop out of its position and cause excruciating pain and discomfort. I decided to request from the team leader a chair to sit on, as I had found that sitting on the floor was becoming unbearable and extremely uncomfortable.

I had to explain myself as to why I needed the chair and it was evident that the team leader was reluctant to provide a chair for me as I would be using it for the duration of every meditation session that we had to attend, and there were a lot of those sessions. Every day without fail we had to meditate six times a day. We had meditation sessions scheduled first thing at 4 am, followed by sessions after morning tea, before lunch, after lunch, before dinner, after dinner and then before bedtime. This process and stringent procedure continued for eleven days straight and there weren't any changes or deviations to the program.

When and if you chose to speak with Judy (the nun) you would have to whisper your requirements or needs into the team leader's ear, and then you were guided on how to act on the spot or later on in the day.

The team leader was a lady who was everywhere. Somehow she knew if you weren't where you were supposed to be at. She knew if you were in your cabin or not. She knew if you spoke or didn't make any form of gestures to others. She just knew.

On the third day of my stay, I had this incredible urge to leave and go home. I began feeling guilty about leaving my family behind during the school holidays and I remember feeling a little bit selfish about having this time away on my own for myself. It was unheard of and I doubted my decision to come to this restful place – at the time I thought that I had made the wrong decision. So I decided to do something about my thoughts and emotions and simply ask that I be granted permission to leave.

I whispered to my team leader that I would like a meeting with Judy the nun, and that I was having doubts about my presence at this place, and would prefer to leave and be at home with my family.

The team leader advised me that I had to schedule an appointment with Judy and that she would make herself available to see me – she would speak to Judy about my request.

My response and thought at the time was simply to say to myself, 'Yeah whatever, do what you have to do, that's fine.' However, it wasn't until the following day when the team leader found me and whispered in my ear, 'Judy will see you at 2 pm today at the meditation hall.'

I thought, 'Okay, no problem.' I had nowhere else to go at 2 pm on that day, so that would be fine.

So 2 pm came. It was after lunch and meditation that I had to see her. I remember opening the entrance to the hall and seeing Judy sit up on her altar, right up at the front of the hall. I had to walk down this long red piece of carpet, and only when the team leader said I could. Therefore, I was waiting on her command as to when I could enter the room and approach Judy, the nun.

That walk was the most distant walk I had ever done in my life. Everything seemed to go in slow motion and it was as if everything around me had frozen. My walking was played in slow motion, frame by frame. It was really a very surreal and unique experience.

As I approached Judy, I could feel my heart beating to the point where I could almost hear it beating. I began to perspire and I felt nervous. Judy was sitting in her meditative position with her eyes closed. She then opened her eyes and finally made eye contact with me. She asked me to sit down. I sat on a blue pillow in front of her.

For a split second it was as if she was reading me like a book, as if she already knew what I was going to say. As if I already knew how the conversation was going to end even before the conversation started. The power that resonated from this woman's soul was huge.

There was only one other time in my life when I'd felt this experience and that was when I met a medium named Kerry Kulken, who believed she could network with people from the other side. She too had power over my soul but only for a split second, as I remember consciously avoiding her eyes.

When Kerry glanced at me for the first time, it seemed and felt evil, with no good-intentioned outcomes, which is why I remember feeling forced to look away from her spellbinding eyes and remove myself by force to ensure that I not maintain any eye contact with her. I was forced to keep my eyes fixated on the tip of her nose to avoid eye contact with her. I literally felt spellbound. Kerry continued to speak to me and I was compelled to listen out of politeness. She also hung onto our handshake and wouldn't let go. As if she had a grasp of me and aimed to control me, my soul and my mind.

Weird, I know. I mean, who believes in witchcraft stuff anyway? Well it would seem that I did and I still do. Nowadays, I call it deception by the devil – or in her case, Satan himself working through her spirit. Somehow I knew that. I didn't understand it all at the time but I knew that this was a powerful lady with some sort of spiritual power over other people. Crazy, I know.

I had to be honest with Judy and advise her that I was ready to go home now. I mentioned to her how I felt extremely guilty about leaving my husband and family behind, especially that it was also during school holidays that I committed to attend the retreat. I explained to Judy that I had made a mistake and that I don't belong here, I should be home with the kids.

Judy listened empathetically and was sitting in silence for some time before she responded to my request. She asked me why I thought I had attended the place to begin with.

I explained that because I had experienced an overwhelm of deaths and grief around me, I didn't feel like I was myself anymore. I felt that I had to get away somewhere for a break and some thinking time.

She acknowledged that my family is important to me and she also pointed out how well they were being looked after while I wasn't there. She clarified that my husband, the children's father, was looking after them. They were being fed, clothed and were safe.

I couldn't have agreed with her more. So I didn't have much to say after that.

Judy proceeded to advise that it was best I stay a little longer before deciding to depart. She explained how my brain was actually experiencing surgery but in a non-intrusive manner and also on a spiritual level.

I had no idea what she was talking about as I had never experienced anything like this encounter before. I agreed with her, aimed to understand what she was suggesting was happening to me and agreed to stay a little longer. Judy added at the end of our conversation that if I felt the need to leave again, I should reschedule another appointment with her to have another discussion; if I felt that I wanted to go then, then she would agree to it and I would be free to go.

Notice I used the word free in the last sentence. This word will be important further on.

Our meeting had ended. I said thank you. She closed her eyes and stayed in her meditative state on the pillow.

I picked myself off the floor, slowly found my balance and walked out quietly from the meditation hall.

Upon leaving the building I can recall my little voice (ego) appearing in my head, advising me that I'd committed to stay a few more days and that I would evaluate my time as each day passed by.

By day six of my stay I felt very pleased with myself and glad that Judy suggested for me to stay for a few more days to see how I went.

As the days and nights went by and all I had to do was walk, eat, meditate and sleep – I had absolutely nothing to think about. I had an empty mindset. I felt relieved that my mind felt so free and at peace. There was no chatter going on in my head – I'm not referring to other voices as if I suffered from schizophrenia, but just the ability to not think of work tasks, groceries, preparations for my children, my husband, my children's activities, my husband's work status, bills or significant people passing on. Simply, not thinking about everything in my life and for once having the opportunity to be silent in my mind. I was feeling relieved with my mindset and thoughts.

My mind was in complete isolation with no worries and no direction other than quietness and peace. I felt this abundance of love for myself and a huge gratification for all living things around me.

I remember sitting on a rock and watching this ant walk the path that I had walked for days, although for the ant it would've taken a mile longer to get to where I was at. The ant looked as if it was on a serious mission and I began to really notice what it was doing. It walked over to another rock that was twice its size. It picked the rock up with its little antennas and moved it to the side. I then noticed something really miraculous. I noticed another little ant climbing its way out of the rockery to get on top of the rock that it appeared to have been stuck under. The first ant that removed the bigger rock in the first place waited for the little ant to get right out of the way before returning the rock to its rightful place.

I was so surprised and amazed at what I had just seen; often I wish I could have taken a 'selfie' of my reaction to that because my face would've said it all. However, as we were forbidden to talk to others, make any face gestures with others, and were strictly forbidden to maintain any eye contact with others, I couldn't share this experience with anyone but myself.

Then, not long after the moment I like to refer to as the 'ant inspiration', I began to notice other amazing things, but this time they were in the trees. I saw with my eyes what looked like silhouettes in the trees – they were all dancing, and posing as if they were to have a photo taken of themselves. I realised again that my eyes were not deceiving me and this place was now sharing some amazing enlightenment, working within my spiritual mindset and soul.

I started to understand the importance of giving Vipassana and the retreat centre a chance. I began to understand why I was experiencing mental surgery in a non-intrusive manner. My mind was becoming healed and had settled from all that I had experienced.

Everywhere I look from that day onwards, I see things that I would never have imagined possible. It's as if I am seeing life through a different perspective. As if life is sharing this with me. As if all that I'm seeing is shared for me to learn from, to understand that life is all around us – and everything we hear, see and touch is real and made of beauty.

Vipassana taught me about beauty for all of us to see,

embrace, love and be grateful for, and to simply understand and appreciate what we are all exposed to daily.

I was also fortunate to see amazing pictures in the sky, all relevant to my time there. If only I had a camera to capture what I saw and share these sights with others. And yet, I have also come to understand that I saw what I did at the time because of my learning and newfound appreciation of my life and my purpose of living – and of those who have passed on. Perhaps the beauty and paradise that they have entered into in the afterlife is the same beauty that is around us, when we really notice things around us that we wouldn't normally notice.

I understand that people who have died are living in paradise if they too were at peace with themselves.

The creation that is our world is absolutely amazing.

On day ten, after experiencing such an abundance of enlightenment, I was ready to go home. I asked if I could have a meeting with Judy once again, following the previous procedure.

Judy was happy to speak with me. The same process occurred. Judy was sitting on her pillow in the meditation hall and I waited patiently for her to request of me to attend and be ready to speak with me.

I walked over and then was asked to sit down. I began our conversation with a deep, sincere thank you and explained how grateful and fortunate I was to have had this experience. I was able to explain all that I had learned and deliver my gratitude to the highest level of praise.

I requested if I could go home that evening because I knew I was ready to do so and I really wanted to be with my family now.

I had longed for their love and had missed them all so dearly.

Judy advised that there were a few more meditation cycles to go through before I could leave and that I would have to wait at least until the silence was lifted before I could depart.

I asked how long I would have to wait for this to occur. Judy advised that it was to happen that afternoon.

I requested if I could fast-track my meditation cycles by sitting alone and completing that cycle, so that by the afternoon when the silence was lifted, there would still be enough daylight for me to drive home safely and reunite with my family, rather than waiting until morning for another sleepover and then be allowed to depart.

She granted my request. Judy placed me in the smaller meditation room. I was to sit in front of the DVD player and go through the final meditation process.

At this point, I was left alone in the room. I realised there were about another twenty-one cycles of meditation to go through. I felt at this point that I was really satisfied and healed and I simply wanted to leave.

I understood that I was meant to be at Vipassana for eleven days, not ten. But in my mind my time was completed and I was ready to go home.

I did the unforgiveable thing at this point. I decided to write a note and leave it on the armchair where it would visible for Judy and her assistant to find. I had a white piece of paper that was the size of a post-it note. I had so much to write yet very little space to write it in.

I began to think carefully about what I could write that clearly stated I was ready to go home and my time at the retreat had to come to an end, as I was well and truly ready to reunite with my family.

So I wrote:

> *Dear Judy,*
>
> *Thank you so much for allowing me the opportunity to obtain clarity for my thoughts, my feelings and my visions. The time I have had here has been extremely rewarding and I now understand the meaning and quality of life, what to truly focus my energy and thoughts on, what is important in life and what it is that I need to value more and have less of. All of this learning came from simply allowing my mind to stop and think or not think and to simply see, believe, feel and experience the enlightenment that I have.*
>
> *Thank you, with kindest regards,*
>
> *Nikki.*

I left the note and began to think how I was going to get my keys, mobile phone and purse returned to me, as these items had to be given to the staff at the beginning of the stay and you were advised that they were kept in a safe place.

Fortunately for me, the silence had been lifted and we were now allowed to speak, connect and network with others. We had stories to share; I had insights of others that came to me while meditating in some of my sessions that I wanted to share with them. This was weird in itself but I knew there were messages that I felt I had to pass onto others, so I did. The information passed on made sense to those I shared it with – and once I passed on what I saw, felt and heard during my meditative state, I felt a sense of relief.

I saw a gentleman sitting at a table collecting donations and returning people's personal belongings. I thought, 'Perfect, here is my opportunity to get my personal belongings and leave.'

So I explained that I had spoken to Judy, and it was agreed that upon completing my meditation training earlier than everybody else it would be okay for me to receive my personal belongings, provide my donation and be ready to depart. The gentleman felt that he had to check my information but couldn't find anyone to ask at the time. So he returned to me and provided my personal belongings. I offered my donations, received my receipt and then said to myself, 'This is it, time to go.'

As I went to my cabin, I grabbed my suitcase and proceeded to my vehicle. I placed my suitcase in the boot of my car. I got into my car and said out aloud, 'Sayonara everyone!'

As I drove past the first gate, I noticed up ahead there was another gate and that we were all locked in. I also noticed a rope line that fenced off land for miles. I parked my car and noticed that I couldn't get out – the only way to get out, I felt at the time, was to bust out. So now I felt like a fugitive aiming to escape and the retreat felt like a cult. I so desperately wanted to get out of there.

So I got creative. I found some cutters in the boot of my car and approached the fence. It had a padlock on it. I first attempted to guess the code. No luck. So I began to use the cutters to cut into the padlock. No luck. I then used the same cutters, hoping they would cut the fence gate. Again, no luck there.

I began to panic. All that relaxing state of mind, body and soul went and left. Now I was feeling overwhelmed, angry, scared and determined to get out. I was on a rampage, looking for any tool I could find in my car that would assist me in cutting my way out. I found a knife. I used it to cut the rope that was between a tree trunk and the gate.

I thought I could probably get the car through the gap and I would be home free. So I got back in the car and slowly drove up to the side, between the gate and the tree trunk. I realised at this point it wasn't going to work because my side mirrors were going to get in the way.

I considered trashing the car, knowing that it would scratch the car and damage my mirror, but I decided this was not the right thing to do.

I stopped the car. I slowly reversed only to find that I got bogged down into a small pothole. I was swearing left, right and centre. I was asking for God to help me get out of here as I truly believed I was locked in and now being held in the retreat against my will.

I ran back to find someone who could assist me. I found the girls who were staying with me in my cabin. They advised me that I looked distressed and scared. I told them that we were all held here against our will. I wanted to go home but I couldn't. I told them I wanted to go home and be with my family, but there was a second gate with a padlock on it so nobody could go out. I also discovered endless rope going around this place. This was a cult, not a retreat. I wanted to go and I couldn't.

The ladies aimed to settle me down and reassure me that everything was going to be okay and that they would talk to Judy. I said, 'You tell her that if that gate isn't opened in the next ten minutes that I will be calling the police, so she better have someone come down and open the gate!'

The ladies advised that it was best I wait in my car, so I wandered back up to the car. I had the ignition running and waited angrily for someone to come and open the gate.

I seriously felt like I was in danger, although now I know that I created the experience myself and I was worrying about nothing. If I had only stayed another night I would've been let free, just like everyone else.

I noticed a gentleman coming down and walking towards the second gate. He looked at me; everything from this point was playing in slow motion. He turned his head in disbelief and noticed that I attempted to cut the padlock. He then noticed that I cut the gate and the rope. He opened the gate by using the code.

I had my window slightly open and I was holding the knife in the other hand for my safety. I demanded that he opened the gate and let me out. He began to open the gate and the moment I saw that I could get my car through it, I simply revved the car and zoomed out of there as quickly as I could without even looking back.

I wanted to ring home and explain to my husband what I just experienced, but I noticed that I had very little reception, which meant I had to wait before I could get a proper signal to be able to call home.

I was reflecting on my drive back - what on earth had just happened? I began to ask myself: 'Why did I allow myself to get into the state that I did? Why did I allow myself to panic? Why did I feel that I was trapped? Why did I think that I was in a cult? Why, why, why?' My intention was to attend this place to find peace within my mind, body and soul but after what just had happened, all of the positive experiences had disappeared – until I spoke to God.

I thanked God for keeping me safe, for experiencing all that I had. Every day, every minute, and every encounter was for further personal learning and personal development on a spiritual level.

I am grateful for the experience that I had. I couldn't wait to see my husband and my children and to share my experience with them in lengthy details. I was so pleased for all that I did, all that I saw, all that I felt and all that I heard.

# Conclusion

Learning to become comfortable with who we are, and what our true purpose in life is, can take a lifetime and can also be missed all together – in particular when we are faced with death, something yet to come for us all.

The discovery of who we can become is truly a lifelong learning process. There are so many varied life experiences that we all have on our journeys, which shape us and provide us with fundamental beliefs and values in our lives.

Some experiences in people's lives can be shared with others when they occur and some are simply stored away, hoping to be left behind and never to be thought about ever again. That is, until a change of mindset occurs and it changes everything about your perception, beliefs and values in your life.

I consider my journey to be meaningful to others, more now than I ever have, and I have finally been able to discuss secrets that have been hidden in the past for over thirty years.

I look forward to sharing with you my spiritual journey, which will be the next chapter of my life that I wish to share for others to learn and grow. In discovering all that I have to date, it has all contributed to a better version of self and truly understanding who I am and my worth on this planet as we know it.

I have come to the realisation that everything I have experienced in the past has been for a purpose. In this life, both in my mortal body and as a spiritual being, I am floating through a journey of experiences.

I am continuing to build new foundations, new patterns of behaviour, new beliefs, new attitudes and new values within my mindset – spiritually, consciously and unconsciously.

I have been able to develop an awareness of becoming a better version of self, and more importantly becoming a character that is 'Christ-like'.

I aim to be someone who is kind, generous, giving, sharing, open to new ideas and willing to be challenged. I am willing to be judged and accept the outcomes, learning to respond and react to different scenarios each and every day, every morning, every hour. I aim to always be tested and commanded to ask the right questions. Is this right for me? Will this serve a purpose? For who? When? Why? What outcomes will I expect to have if I do this? What will it all look like once it's said and dealt with? How will I feel? Will I experience joyfulness? Will I experience happiness? Will this truly work for others and for myself?

Always seeking clarity and answers is a great attribute to have, and if I knew this back then, I may have made better choices and not have experienced all that I had.

I believe I have become all that I ever wanted to become, and that was to be successful; I can freely say that I am. I have been given a life to live and when I ask great questions and make great decisions, I will be led by fantastic outcomes that are measurable and rewarding.

I wake up every day and I can breathe.

I wake up in the mornings and I can dress myself.

I wake up ready to pray and be grateful for all that I have and for what the day will bring.

I act on intuition that feels right for me – without fear, without guilt, without any unnerving surprises.

I am able to make better choices that feel right.

I am able to give, share, offer all that I can and measure my success based on all that I have to support with, using the resources that are available to me at the time.

I have a family that is supportive and that loves me unconditionally.

I have a purpose for living, and that is the learning that comes with the journey and the experiences that are still yet to come.

We cannot stop time until time for us is ready to stop, and that will happen when it's meant to happen. Therefore, we can simply keep on moving towards events that serve a purpose for others and ourselves. Creating and making a difference in people's lives will then ultimately create and make a difference in our own lives.

We were created to live a life full of joy and happiness, full of an abundance of unconditional love. I have that!

What we have in front of us can be precious – and when we are ready to notice things that we hadn't noticed before, perceptions differ. The beauty around us daily becomes more noticeable to the human eye. The trees, the clouds, the grass, the butterflies flying in the air, the warmth of the sun on our faces and so forth.

We are all on a journey aiming to discover why things happen to us. Seeking answers, and making choices that impact our lives.

Once we have an awareness of who we truly are – what we have to be grateful for and how we can become a better version of ourselves – only then have we truly become our masterful selves, which is an ultimate way of thinking and living, feeling humble and complete within our soul.

Life will continue to present challenges. I have learnt that now, and understand that the challenges presented are for us to learn something from the events that occur. We don't know what we don't know, until we know it.

I have come to understand that success for me is measured by my spiritual well-being, which is aligned with my mindset, body and soul.

If what I do brings joy to others then it will also bring happiness and joy to me. This is a good motto that I have manifested into my beliefs and encourage others to do the same.

I urge any person who may have experienced anything like I have – be that rape, abortion, suicidal thoughts, confusion, heartache, deception – to reach out for help and to seek guidance and support from a source that we may not comprehend. I urge you to hope.

Perhaps believe in something that is greater than you. Have faith in something and believe that you are doing the best you can with the resources you have at the time.

Always seek clarity and a better outcome; ask big questions to yourself and to others. All of this thinking will lead to you becoming a better version of yourself.

NLP Coaching has become part of my life. With the resources I now have in hand, I have successfully added fantastic value to my life, my husband's life and my children's lives. I contribute to the lives of the people who ask for guidance and who want to become better versions of themselves.

Creating changes for the better is what we all should be striving for as part of our humanity – let's all rejoice and make it so.

It all starts with you being able to let go and move on.

www.ingramcontent.com/pod-product-compliance
Lightning Source LLC
Chambersburg PA
CBHW032222010526
44113CB00032B/426